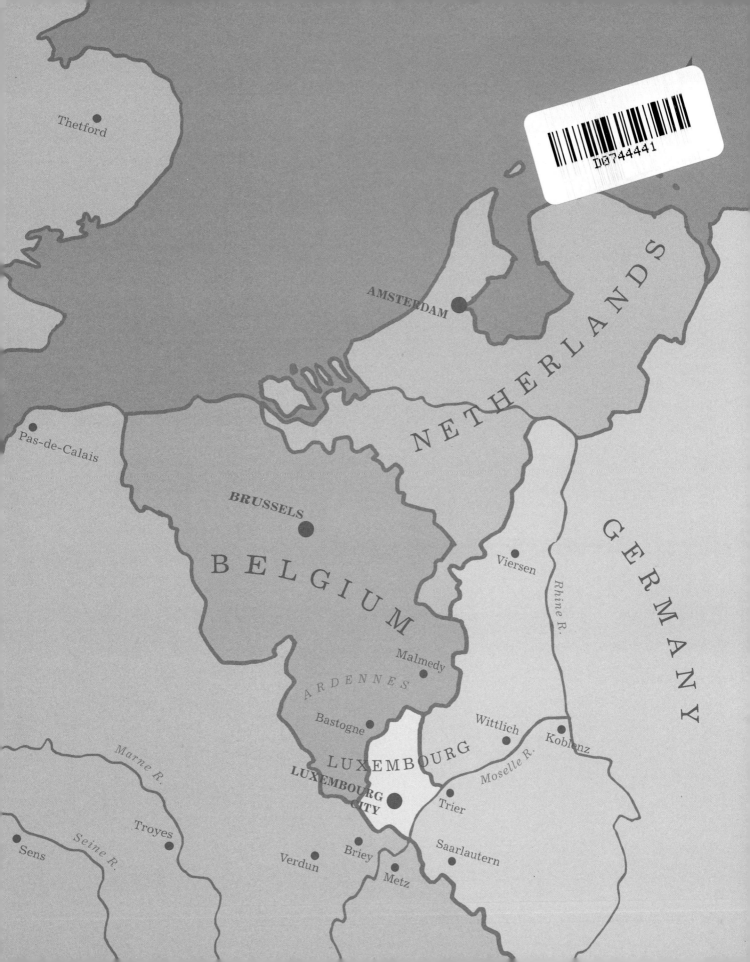

Thetford

AMSTERDAM

NETHERLANDS

Pas-de-Calais

BRUSSELS

BELGIUM

Viersen

GERMANY

Rhine R.

Malmedy

ARDENNES

Bastogne

Wittlich

Koblenz

Moselle R.

LUXEMBOURG

Marne R.

LUXEMBOURG
CITY

Trier

Troyes

Saarlautern

Sens

Seine R.

Verdun

Briey

Metz

PRAISE FOR *THE GHOST ARMY OF WORLD WAR II*

World War II was the greatest event in the history of mankind, and although it has been the subject of countless books, documentaries, and academic courses, there is so much still to know. *The Ghost Army of World War II* describes a perfect example of a little-known, highly imaginative, and daring maneuver that helped open the way for the final drive to Germany. It is a riveting tale told through personal accounts and sketches along the way—ultimately, a story of success against great odds. I enjoyed it enormously.

TOM BROKAW

Journalist and author of *The Greatest Generation*

Brings to life a whale of a tale of World War II innovation—one laced with brash creativity. The notion of a special Army unit using dummy equipment, mobile loudspeakers, officer impersonations, and foul rumors to deceive German forces seems outlandish, but the tactics worked. This theater-goes-to-war story is finely told and beautifully illustrated—an important contribution.

GORDON H. "NICK" MUELLER

President and CEO, The National WWII Museum

The Ghost Army of World War II is a veritable hive of fascinating information based on sound research. It's apparent that Rick Beyer and Elizabeth Sayles enjoy the subject with a level of dedication and passion that warms the hearts of irascible military historians such as me. I heartily recommend this book.

MARTIN KING

Author of *Voices of the Bulge* and *The Tigers of Bastogne*, consultant to the History Channel

A fascinating read, and a fun one as well. *Audacious* is the right word for this daring sideshow that protected Patton's flank and other American soldiers. The original art is superb and frequently humorous. A well-crafted account of the amazing combination of shenanigans and tremendous courage that characterized the Twenty-Third Headquarters Special Troops.

LIBBY O'CONNELL

Chief historian of the History Channel, author of *The American Plate: A Culinary History in 100 Bites*

The GHOST ARMY
of WORLD WAR II

Inflatable dummy tanks and trucks set up near the Rhine River in Germany, 1945. Even the tire tracks were faked.

Military deception is much like a successful magic trick. It is about fooling people into believing that something is happening that isn't.

The
GHOST ARMY
of WORLD WAR II

How One Top-Secret Unit
Deceived the Enemy
with Inflatable Tanks,
Sound Effects,
and Other Audacious Fakery

RICK BEYER & ELIZABETH SAYLES

Princeton Architectural Press ★ New York

CONTENTS

INTRODUCTION

THE CECIL B. DeMILLE WARRIORS

Its complement was more theatrical than military.
It was like a traveling road show
that went up and down the front lines.

— Official History of the 23rd Headquarters Special Troops

They drove east from Paris, leaving the City of Light behind and hurrying into the inky darkness that soon enveloped the blacked-out French roads. The convoy of half-tracks, trucks, and jeeps moved relentlessly through the night, stopping only briefly before resuming the journey in the gray dawn light. By midday on September 15, 1944, the men of the Twenty-Third Headquarters Special Troops had traveled 250 miles and were moving into position along the Moselle River, near the border between Luxembourg and Germany. The weather was cold and rainy, presaging a winter that would be called the worst in forty years. The GIs were understandably edgy: the German lines were said to be less than two miles to the east, just across the river. "We're the only outfit on this part of the front except for one cavalry squadron spread very thinly," wrote Sergeant Bob Tompkins in his diary. "No one knows where [the] front is." They had been rushed here from Paris to perform a vital but dangerous job code-named Operation Bettembourg.

Their mission was to put on a show, with the German Army as the audience.

They were plugging a hole in General George Patton's line by pretending to be the Sixth Armored Division, with all its tanks and might. But the men of the Twenty-Third had no tanks—no real ones, anyway—and precious little might. In fact, they carried no weapon heavier than a .50-caliber machine gun. This cast of artists, designers, radio operators, and engineers was equipped instead with battalions of rubber dummies, a world-class collection of sound-effects records, and all the creativity the soldiers could muster. They understood all too well that their own lives depended on the quality of their performance—if the

All the different dummy vehicles used by the Ghost Army

Germans saw through their deception, they could attack and overrun the small, lightly armed unit. "There was nothing but our hopes and prayers that separated us from a panzer division," Lieutenant Bob Conrad recalled. But thousands of other lives were at stake as well. If the Germans realized how thinly held the sector was, they could break through and attack Patton from the rear.

In other words, it was just another day in the life for the men of what became known as the Ghost Army.

This top-secret unit went into action in June 1944, a few weeks after D-Day. For the next nine months they conducted deception missions from Normandy to the Rhine River. "Its complement was more theatrical than military," noted the unit's official US Army history. "It was like a traveling road show that went up and down the front lines impersonating the real fighting outfits."

What they did was so secret that few of their fellow American soldiers even knew they were there. Yet they pulled off twenty-one different deceptions and are credited with saving thousands of lives through stagecraft and sleight of hand. Like actors in a repertory theater, they would ask themselves: "Who are we this time?" Then they would put on a multimedia show tailored to that particular deception, often operating dangerously close to the front lines. They threw themselves into their impersonations, sometimes setting up phony command posts and masquerading as generals. They frequently put themselves in danger, suffering casualties as a consequence. After holding Patton's line along the Moselle, they barely escaped capture by the Germans in the Battle of the Bulge, and in March 1945 they performed their most dazzling deception, misleading the Germans about where two American divisions would cross the Rhine River.

Their mission bordered on the surreal. But that is only part of their amazing story. The artists in the unit, recruited to handle visual

(opposite) Some of the eleven hundred men of the Ghost Army

deception, used their spare time to chronicle the unit's adventures in thousands of paintings and drawings, creating a unique and poignant visual record of their war. After coming home many took up postwar careers as painters, sculptors, designers, illustrators, or architects. A surprising number went on to become famous, including fashion designer Bill Blass, painter and sculptor Ellsworth Kelly, and wildlife artist Arthur Singer.

Thirty years after the war, when the details of their story were still being kept secret, a United States Army analyst who studied their missions came away deeply impressed with the impact of their illusions. "Rarely, if ever, has there been a group of such a few men which had so great an influence on the outcome of a major military campaign."

They were the "Cecil B. DeMille Warriors," in the words of Ghost Army veteran Dick Syracuse.

This is their story.

Sergeant Joseph Mack, one of the many artists in the Ghost Army, used this lozenge box to hold his paints.

Dummy tank "hidden" so it can still be seen

1

MY CON ARTISTS

The con-artist's job is to hoodwink the enemy
instead of slugging it out with him.

— Ralph Ingersoll

Every army practices deception.
If they don't, they can't win,
and they know it.
— General Wesley Clark, United States Army

Ralph Ingersoll had the perfect combination of attributes to be a deception planner. Not only was he a genuinely creative thinker, he was also a bold, confident dissembler. "I've never met anyone who was such a bright guy who was such a goddamned liar," fellow deception planner Went Eldredge later told Ingersoll biographer Roy Hoopes. "He'd say anything to get what he wanted." Ingersoll is the only person to have claimed credit for dreaming up the idea of the Ghost Army. Given his reputation, it is easy to be skeptical. But he was certainly there when it happened, and even if he didn't think up the idea all on his own, he undoubtedly provided a good share of the creative spark.

Before the war Ralph Ingersoll was a celebrity journalist and best-selling author—not to mention a man who attracted controversy as effortlessly as a starlet draws paparazzi. A product of Hotchkiss prep school and Yale University, he became managing editor of the *New Yorker*, publisher of *Fortune*, and general manager of Time Inc. He was one of the prime movers in the launching of *Life* magazine but made many enemies. He left Time to found his own innovative and left-leaning newspaper in New York, called *PM*. In a front-page editorial, Ingersoll wrote of *PM*, "We're against people who push other people around." The *New York Times* once described him as "a prodigiously energetic egotist with a talent for making magazines, covering a war, womanizing—and pushing other people around." He acted as a star reporter for his

Ralph Ingersoll

own paper, met face-to-face with Joseph Stalin and Winston Churchill, hung out at the White House with FDR, and made good copy for other reporters.

Ingersoll was in his forties when war broke out. After complaining vociferously when inducted by his local draft board (Ingersoll thought publishers should be exempt), he eventually gave in and joined up. Entering the army as a private, he quickly won a commission and became a staff officer. He served in North Africa, then came home and wrote a best-selling book, *The Battle Is the Pay-Off*. In the second half of 1943 Captain Ingersoll was stationed in the Operations branch of the army's headquarters in London. He worked alongside British planners on various strategic deceptions so that American activities would dovetail with the overall British plan.

He took to deception like a duck to water. "For Ingersoll, it became love at first sight," wrote Sefton Delmer, a British counterintelligence officer who authored the memoir *The Counterfeit Spy*. "He became one of the foremost American exponents of the art of deception." He was full of ideas to meet any contingency. "Any problem, he would just think a bit and come out with something," said Went Eldredge, who in civilian life taught at Dartmouth. "This was damn irritating for a college professor. He was always three moves ahead of you."

One of the British deceptions Ingersoll worked on was Operation Fortitude, a massive effort designed to fool the Germans about where the D-Day landings would take place. Many means of deception— including inflatable landing craft, turned spies, and phony radio transmissions—were used to convince the Germans that an army under General George Patton was preparing to invade France at the Pas-de-Calais, when the real invasion would take place in Normandy.

In late 1943, according to an unpublished account Ingersoll wrote years later, this collaboration with British deceivers led him to the idea of creating a tactical deception unit flexible enough to create numerous different battlefield illusions. "My prescription was for a battalion that could imitate a whole corps of either armor or infantry…a super secret battalion of specialists in the art of manipulating our antagonists' decisions." He referred to the unit as "my con artists," and said its creation was "my only original contribution to my country's armed forces." He went on to say: "When I first dreamed it up, I considered it one of my more improbable dreams, but damned if the Pentagon planners didn't buy it whole."

Ingersoll had a reputation for exaggerating his accomplishments. John Shaw Billings, who worked with him at Time, complained "he blew his own horn in the most outrageous way." And he certainly didn't conceive of the Ghost Army all on his own. One of his most important collaborators was his immediate superior, Colonel Billy Harris.

In many ways, Harris was the polar opposite of the flamboyant Ingersoll. He was a buttoned-up, straight-arrow West Point military man. He came from a family steeped in military tradition. His father was a general. His uncle was a general. Harris would himself eventually become a general. His mother, Lulu Harris, introduced Dwight D. Eisenhower, then a young army lieutenant, to his future wife, Mamie Doud, at Fort Sam Houston in 1916. Ingersoll called Harris a "cocky little man" and thought he had "more cheek than imagination." Nevertheless, the two worked well together. While Ingersoll was full of wild, pie-in-the-sky ideas, Harris had the military training and discipline needed to implement deception in a way that could actually work.

Inflatable dummy tank

The plan they developed, with input from other military planners, was to create a unit of about eleven hundred men capable of impersonating one or two infantry or armored divisions—the equivalent of twenty to forty times their number. "It's really simple," Corporal Sebastian Messina explained to a reporter from the *Worcester Daily Telegram* shortly after the war was over. "Suppose the Umpteenth Division is holding a certain sector. Well, we move in, secretly of course, and they move out. We then faithfully ape the Umpteenth in everything....Then the Umpteenth, which the Boches [the Germans] think is in front of them, is suddenly kicking them in the pants ten miles to the rear." Ralph Ingersoll thought that *deception* was the wrong word

The inflatable personnel developed for deception purposes did not see much use because their lack of movement was such a giveaway.

for what they did. "The right one should be *manipulation*—the art and practice of manipulating your enemies' mental processes so that they come to a false conclusion about what you are up to."

Military deception—or manipulation—has a long history, going back to the Trojan Horse. "Every army practices deception," says retired United States Army General Wesley Clark, former commander of NATO and a student of military history. "If they don't, they can't win, and they know it." American generals have often used it to gain an advantage. Seemingly caught in a British trap in January 1777, General George Washington detailed a small number of men to tend bonfires and make digging noises to make it seem as if he were readying for battle in the morning, while in fact he was spiriting most of his troops away to attack the British rear. In 1862 Confederate General Joseph E. Johnston used log cannons to make his front line in northern Virginia appear to be bristling with guns and too strong for the Union to attack. Earlier in World War II, the British had made deft use of deception in North Africa.

But the Ghost Army wasn't simply more of the same. It represented something unique in the history of war. George Rebh, who served in the unit as a captain and retired a major general, described it as nothing less than the first unit in the history of warfare that was dedicated solely to deception. "Now, you take Napoleon and Lee and Caesar," said Rebh. "They would take part of their fighting force and use them for deception, but when they got through, they would come back as fighting force. In contrast, our sole mission was deception."

The Ghost Army was different in two other ways. It was designed to project multimedia deceptions, using visual, sonic, and radio illusions together so that however the enemy was gathering information, everything would point to the same false picture. And it was mobile, capable of carrying out a deception for a few days in one place, packing it up, and moving on to someplace else to carry out a completely different deception. In effect, a commander could maneuver the Twenty-Third the same way he would a real unit.

An idea of this magnitude had to get approval from the highest levels. General Jake Devers, top American commander in the European theater of operations, embraced the idea and gave the go-ahead in a memo to Washington on Christmas Eve, 1943. Military historian Jonathan Gawne, author of *Ghosts of the ETO*, has argued that Devers deserves the lion's share of the credit for the creation of the Ghost Army. "Lots of people suggest things," he said, "but it was Devers that had his name on the bottom of the memo and thus his butt on the line." Once General Dwight D. Eisenhower replaced Devers in January 1945, he, too, became an enthusiastic supporter of the endeavor.

The new unit was officially activated on January 20, 1944, at Camp Forrest, Tennessee. To carry out the deception mission, the army brought together three existing units and one brand-new one, placing them all under the command of Colonel Harry L. Reeder (who would continue to command the Twenty-Third Headquarters Special Troops until the unit returned home from Europe at the end of the war):

The 603rd Engineer Camouflage Battalion Special

This was the largest unit in the Ghost Army, with 379 men. These visual deceivers, also known as *camoufleurs*, used an array of inflatable rubber tanks, trucks, artillery, and jeeps to create deceptive tableaux for enemy aerial reconnaissance or distant observers. The unit had spent the previous two years doing camouflage work and included in its ranks many artists specially recruited for that job.

The Signal Company Special

Formerly the 244th Signal Company, this group of 296 men carried out radio deception, also called "spoof radio." Operators created phony traffic nets, impersonating radio operators from real units. They mastered the art of mimicking an operator's method of sending Morse code, to prevent the enemy from realizing that the real unit and its radio operator were long gone.

The 3132 Signal Service Company Special

This sonic deception unit was staffed with 145 men. Their mission was to play sound effects from powerful speakers mounted on half-tracks (armored vehicles with wheels in the front and tracks in the back), to simulate the sounds of units moving and operating at night. Recently formed, they had been undergoing training at the Army Experimental Station at Pine Camp (now Fort Drum) in upstate New York when the Twenty-Third was assembled and would join them later in England.

The 406th Engineer Combat Company Special

Led by Captain George Rebh, the 168 men of the 406th were trained as fighting soldiers. They provided perimeter security for the rest of the Ghost Army. They also executed construction and demolition tasks, including digging tank and artillery positions. The men of the 406th frequently used their bulldozers to simulate tank tracks as part of the visual deception.

THE UNIT

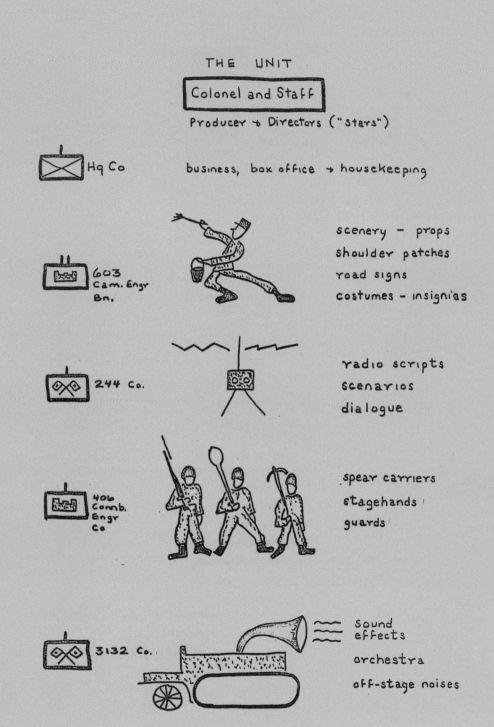

Colonel and Staff

Producer & Directors ("stars")

Hq Co — business, box office & housekeeping

603 Cam. Engr Bn. — scenery - props / shoulder patches / road signs / costumes - insignias

244 Co. — radio scripts / scenarios / dialogue

406 Comb. Engr Co — spear carriers / stagehands / guards

3132 Co. — Sound effects / orchestra / off-stage noises

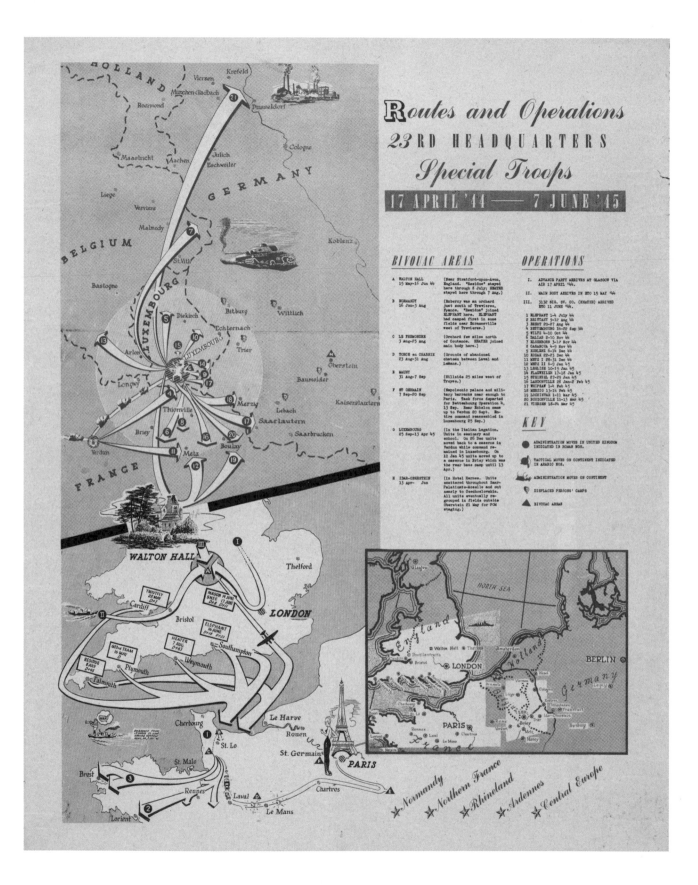

These four units, plus a headquarters company—eleven hundred men in all—were capable of simulating two divisions—approximately thirty thousand men—to confuse and confound the enemy. The Twenty-Third eventually came under the direct command of General Omar Bradley's Twelfth United States Army Group, carrying out operations planned by Bradley's Special Plans Branch—under Billy Harris and Ralph Ingersoll.

The biggest of the four units brought together for the deception mission was the 603rd Camouflage Engineers. It was an unusual unit, rumored to have the highest average IQ of any unit in the army. But what really made it unique was that it was loaded with some of the most unmilitary people imaginable—artists.

BIVOUAC AREAS

A WALTON HALL
15 May–16 Jun 44
(Near Stratford-upon-Avon, England. "Residue" stayed here through 8 July; HEATER stayed here through 7 Aug.)

B NORMANDY
16 Jun–3 Aug
(Bubercy was an orchard just south of Trevieres, France. "Residue" joined ELEPHANT here. ELEPHANT had camped first in some fields near Ecrammeville west of Trevieres.)

C LE FREMONDRE
3 Aug–23 Aug
(Orchard few miles north of Coutance. HEATER joined main body here.)

D TORCE en CHARNIE
23 Aug–31 Aug
(Grounds of abandoned chateau between Laval and LeMans.)

E MAUNY
31 Aug–7 Sep
(Hillside 25 miles west of Troyes.)

F ST GERMAIN
7 Sep–20 Sep
(Napoleonic palace and military barracks near enough to Paris. Task force departed for Bettembourg Operation 4, 13 Sep. Rear Echelon came up to Verdun 20 Sept. Entire command reassembled in Luxembourg 25 Sep.)

G LUXEMBOURG
25 Sep–13 Apr 45
(In the Italian Legation. Units in seminary and school. On 26 Dec units moved back to a caserne in Verdun while command remained in Luxembourg. On 10 Jan 45 units moved up to a caserne in Briey which was the rear base camp until 13 Apr.)

H IDAR-OBERSTEIN
13 Apr– Jun
(In Hotel Hermes. Units scattered throughout Saar-Palatinate-Moselle and out nearly to Czechoslovakia. All units eventually regrouped in fields outside Oberstein 21 May for POM staging.)

OPERATIONS

I. ADVANCE PARTY ARRIVES AT GLASGOW VIA AIR 17 APRIL '44.

II. MAIN BODY ARRIVES IN ETO 15 MAY '44

III. 3132 SIG. SV. CO. (HEATER) ARRIVED ETO 11 JUNE '44.

1 ELEPHANT 1–4 July 44
2 BRITTANY 9–12 Aug 44
3 BREST 20–27 Aug 44
4 BETTEMBOURG 14–22 Sep 44
5 WILTZ 4–10 Oct 44
6 DALIAS 2–10 Nov 44
7 ELSENBORN 3–12 Nov 44
8 CASANOVA 4–9 Nov 44
9 KOBLENZ 6–14 Dec 44
10 KODAK 22–23 Dec 44
11 METZ I 28–31 Dec 44
12 METZ II 6–9 Jan 45
13 LEGLISE 10–15 Jan 45
14 FLAXWEILER 17–18 Jan 45
15 STEINSEL 27–29 Jan 45
16 LANDONVILLE 28 Jan–2 Feb 45
17 WHIPSAW 1–4 Feb 45
18 MERZIG 13–14 Feb 45
19 LOCHINVAR 1–11 Mar 45
20 BOUZONVILLE 11–13 Mar 45
21 VIERSEN 18–24 Mar 45

KEY

● ADMINISTRATION MOVES IN UNITED KINGDOM INDICATED IN ROMAN NOS.

TACTICAL MOVES ON CONTINENT INDICATED IN ARABIC NOS.

ADMINISTRATION MOVES ON CONTINENT

DISPLACED PERSONS' CAMPS

▲ BIVOUAC AREAS

New York University students studying camouflage in 1943

2

THE ART BOYS

We were looked on as kind of nutcases
by the hardworking, no-nonsense backbone of America,
the people that worked for a living and didn't sketch.

— Jack Masey

New Recruit by Walter Arnett, 1942

NEW RECRUIT
IN THE BARACKS
RECEPTION CENTER
FT SILL, OKLAHOMA
PVT Richard H Morton '42

Private Ned Harris was only eighteen years old when he reported for duty at Fort Meade, Maryland, in 1942. He was there to join up with the newly formed 603rd Engineer Camouflage Battalion Special. Young and nervous, far from home, he had no idea what to expect. As he signed in, someone asked him where he was from, and he answered, "New York." Then another soldier inquired if he had attended Pratt Institute in Brooklyn.

"I immediately said yes," recalled Harris, "and they began laughing. I didn't know whether to be embarrassed or what. Were they laughing with me or at me?" Then another voice chimed in with words that made Harris feel right at home. "Just another artist arrived to be part of our fraternity." Harris was one of many creative types who had found their way into the 603rd. Many others also came from Pratt. James Boudreau, the dean of Pratt's art school, was a general in the United States Army reserve. In the early 1940s, with war already raging in Europe and Asia and fears rising over the threat of aerial devastation from enemy bombing, the farsighted Boudreau organized an experimental laboratory dedicated to camouflage research and development. He recruited camouflage experts to the faculty and instituted a camouflage course.

Bob Tompkins was quick to sign up for it. He was taking courses at Pratt while also working at an advertising agency in the Chrysler Building for $17.50 a week. Ed Biow, Ellsworth Kelly, George Martin, and William Sayles also

Ray Harford, Bob Boyajian, and Victor Dowd (left to right, seated and looking at camera) illustrating comics at Jack Binder's studio in 1940. They later served together in the Ghost Army.

took the course. They built detailed tabletop models and went out to the Pratt family estate on the North Shore of Long Island to work with camouflage netting. Boudreau, a pilot, would fly overhead and snap photos to show them what their camouflage installations looked like from the air. "Amateuring around," Biow called it, but it led them all into the 603rd.

Kelly's journey to the unit involved an unusual detour. He requested assignment to the 603rd, but when his orders didn't come through, he was transferred to Camp Hale, Colorado, to join the Tenth Mountain Division ski troops. This, in spite of the fact he had never been on skis in his life! When his orders to join the camouflage unit finally arrived, he felt sorry to leave the beautiful mountain camp.

Victor Dowd recalled that Dean Boudreau actively recruited art students (and recent graduates) for newly organized army camouflage battalions. Dowd had known since childhood that he was going to be an artist. "My mother never had to worry about me on rainy days, because I'd occupy myself by drawing." After graduating from Pratt in 1940, he and classmates Ray Harford and Bob Boyajian worked together as

comic-strip artists at Jack Binder's studio during what is now considered the golden age of comics. They drew such heroes as Bulletman, Captain Midnight, and Spy Smasher. Under the auspices of Boudreau, all three found their way into the 603rd.

As did Arthur Shilstone. Unlike Victor Dowd, Shilstone had no intention of being an artist. "I thought the thing to do was to be a businessman, wear a blue suit, someday have the end office." So he took a lot of business courses, in which he did quite poorly. But he excelled in an art course. His art teacher suggested he should think about a career in art. He dutifully went back to his business teachers to see what they thought. He recalled with laughter how enthusiastic they were. "They said, 'That's a great idea, Arthur. You really should go and do something else.'" So he went to Pratt to study illustration and ended up in the 603rd.

John Jarvie was studying at New York's Cooper Union when he enlisted. "It was a big war," recalled Jarvie, "and everybody went." Jarvie heard about the camouflage unit and applied to be a part of it. "You had to write to them, and they had to accept you—it had nothing to do with the army draft at all." Seventeen-year-old freshman Art Kane and twenty-five-year-old graduate Arthur Singer also hailed from Cooper Union. Jack Masey was a recent graduate from the New York High School of Music and Art. Keith Williams was a prizewinning artist in his mid-thirties. Bernie Mason was designing display windows for a store in Philadelphia. Harold Laynor was a recent graduate of the Parsons School of Design, also in New York City. George Vander Sluis had painted post office murals for the WPA and taught art at the Broadmoor Academy in Colorado. Bill Blass was a fledgling fashion designer who

(left) *Ray Harford* by Victor
Dowd, 1945

(right, top) Victor Dowd's
sketchbook, 1944

(right, bottom) *Self-Portrait*
by Arthur Singer, 1944

(top) Camouflage lesson

(bottom) A report handwritten by Bill Blass about the merits of using chicken feathers for camouflage

PFC. Wm. R. Blass

1.

Advantages	Disadvantages
(1) Would be more adaptable to unusual terrains such as snow or sand than burlap etc.	(1) Not always easily obtainable
(2) Lighter in weight, so less wire maybe used than in a fish net or chicken wire flattop.	(2) Due to the sticking factor it would not be easy always to erect a chicken feather flattop in a great hurry.
(3) Durability is amazing	(3) Range of colours is small and dyeing as yet not too successful.
(4) Feathers, being water repelent will not change their appearance in rainy weather as does fabric or paper	

2.

Other possible uses for chicken feathers other than flatops. For one thing in a desert one could erect a very convincing sand dune of grey or beige chicken feathers. Also this would be true in a snow country where an artificial drift of chicken feather snow could hide successfuly several snipers. Perhaps impossible but a thought is covering (directly) tanks & other vechiles with feathers so as to disguise their identity & shapes

Ellsworth Kelly with silk
screens, Fort Meade, 1943

had recently moved to New York from Fort Wayne,
Indiana. They and many other artists filled the ranks of
the 603rd.

After basic training at Fort Meade, they began learning
the ins and outs of camouflage. They experimented with
everything from tin cans to chicken feathers to see what
they would look like to aerial observers. They studied
how to use texture, color, shadow, blending, and shape in
camouflage. Ellsworth Kelly helped to silk-screen posters
that introduced infantry units to these basic camouflage
principles. In later years Kelly was to become famous
for his minimalist painting and sculpture, and art critic
Eugene Goossen argued that this exposure to military
camouflage helped shape Kelly's aesthetic. "The involvement with form and shadow, with the construction and
destruction of the visible…was to affect nearly everything he did in painting and sculpture."

Soon they graduated to larger-scale projects. Fearing
German bomber raids, the army had the unit camouflage coastal
defense artillery on Long Island and at the Glenn L. Martin plant in
Baltimore, where B-26 bombers were made. "Our outfit was responsible
for disguising that and covering it," recalled Ned Harris, "so from the
air it looked like it was the countryside." In 1943 they took part in
large-scale maneuvers in Tennessee.

Camouflaged Glenn L. Martin
plant, Baltimore

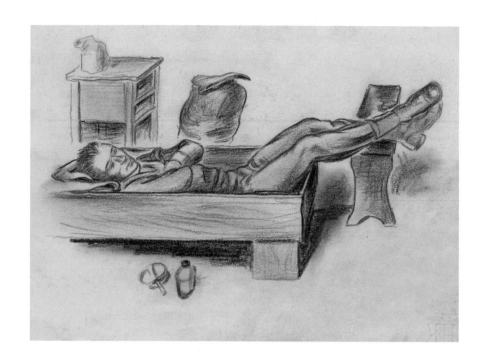

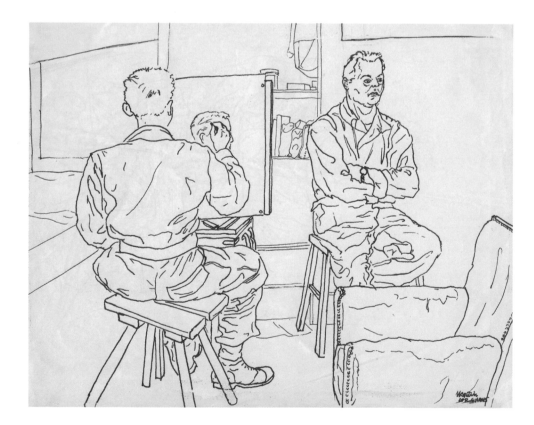

(top left) *Quick Nap* by Tony
Young, 1944

(top right) *Watercolor* by
John Hapgood, 1944

(bottom) *Portrait* by George
Martin, 1945

United States Army Corps of Engineers

Dec. 27, 1943

GI Sketching by Joseph Mack, 1943

But while camouflage was their job, art was their love. The 603rd served as an incubator in which artists could hone their skills. "I learned more about who I was as an artist and…my craft by being there rather than even at school," said Harris, "and it continued till the end."

The artists in the 603rd sketched and painted all sorts of things: their barracks, their buddies, themselves. "It isn't as though we weren't busy," said Victor Dowd. "But you have to realize, no matter how busy a soldier is, there's always down time. Soldiers are playing cards, they're shooting craps, they're reading. And I drew. I just developed the habit, and I don't think it's ever left me." Harold Laynor recalled his first sergeant "was always berating me for taking so much time up with my, as he called it, 'darn painting.'" Laynor thought the sergeant should have expected no different, given that the men were "a mass of artists and architects" who thought they "were going to camouflage the United States."

Not all the soldiers in the 603rd were artists. There were policemen, farmers, accountants, shoe salesmen, and other people from all walks of life. "It was a wild array of all kinds of people," said Arthur Shilstone. For Jack Masey, a kid from Brooklyn, it was an eye-opening experience. "I'd only known Brooklynites or Manhattanites. Now suddenly I was thrown into another world. I was intrigued by the people who constituted this world, their accents, the obscenities they threw out. This was another awakening for me: hey, this is America. It's got all kinds of crazy people in it."

The sharp cultural divide in the unit was obvious to many. Bill Blass marveled that he could hear Beethoven's Fifth at one end of the barracks and "Pistol Packin' Mama" at the other. "And we were looked on as kind of nutcases," said Jack Masey, "by the hardworking, no-nonsense backbone of America, the people that worked for a living and didn't sketch."

Some even thought that the young artists wouldn't be able to hack the army. Not so. "The artists did what everybody else did," said Arthur Shilstone. "They made the hikes and [carried] their rifles and everything else, and they were as good or better than the other guys: the bartenders, the truck drivers, and so forth." In early 1943 Private Harold Dahl, a young sculptor from New Jersey, noted in a letter to his mother that of the twenty sergeants in his company, fifteen were artists. "And some of these tough engineers thought the art boys would be flops!" he added with pride.

In the end, as in countless other army units, the young men of different backgrounds found a way to put aside their differences and work together. "It did pit us against people who probably never knew or met an artist," said Ned Harris, "and knew nothing about the world that was ours. And they learned something from us, and we learned from them."

The 603rd had been together for nearly two years when it was uprooted from Fort Meade in January 1944 and sent to Camp Forrest in Tennessee to be part of the Twenty-Third Headquarters Special Troops. Instead of trying to hide things, they were now going to be in the risky business of drawing attention to themselves. Lieutenant Gil Seltzer, a twenty-nine-year-old New York City architect, concluded that the 603rd was being attached to a "suicide outfit." But Private Dahl, for one, found the new assignment very much to his taste. He wrote home to say that he couldn't talk about what they were going to do, "but it promises to be very interesting and frankly it looks like we are at last going to play a real part in the war effort."

Caricatures of Tony Young,
Max David, and James Steg
by Jack Masey, 1944

Inflatable M-4 Sherman tank

3

MEN OF WILE

You couldn't really believe that what we
were going to do would be effective.
How could we come along with rubber dummies
and blow [them] up and make it look real?

— Irving Stempel

Officers who had once commanded 32-ton tanks, felt
frustrated and helpless with a battalion of rubber M-4s,
93 pounds fully inflated. The adjustment from man of action
to man of wile was most difficult. Few realized at first
that one could spend just as much energy <u>pretending</u> to fight
as actually fighting.

— Official History of the 23rd Headquarters Special Troops

Colonel Harry L. Reeder,
commander of the Twenty-
Third Headquarters Special
Troops

The clock was running as the Twenty-Third Headquarters Special
Troops began to take shape in January 1944. Everyone knew that
the invasion of Europe was only a matter of months away. They had
precious little time during which to get organized and learn their
deception mission. The United States Army had no doctrine for tactical
deception, no book for them to go by. They would have to develop much
of their own training, tactics, techniques, and procedures, and teach
themselves to be deceivers.

The commander of the unit, Colonel Harry L. Reeder, was an old-
school infantry officer who had been serving since World War I. Colonel
Billy Harris and Captain Ralph Ingersoll, in the Special Plans branch,
thought him a poor choice because of his lack of flexibility and recep-
tivity to new ideas. Harris derided Reeder as "an old fud." Reeder, by
all accounts, was none too happy with his assignment, either. On at
least one occasion he suggested to the War Department that the Twenty-
Third should be dissolved, freeing him up to command an infantry regiment. Many of the men who served under him came to regard Reeder as
a narrow-minded military man uninterested in adapting to the unusual
needs of a deception unit.

Lieutenant Colonel Clifford Simenson, the unit's operations officer,
was cut from a different cloth. A protégé of one of the army's highest-
ranking and best-regarded officers, General Leslie McNair, Simenson,
too, had hoped for an infantry command. Upon being assigned to the
Twenty-Third, he initially found himself perplexed about how best
to proceed. "There were no manuals, no instructions, no guidance, and
no orders from higher headquarters except to prepare for overseas

movement." Unlike Reeder, however, Simenson threw himself whole-heartedly into the deception mission. Intelligent and open-minded, he was instrumental in formulating the doctrines and tactics they would employ on the battlefield to simulate larger units under a variety of different conditions.

Surprisingly, for such a small unit, there were a number of other lieutenant colonels and majors, many of them West Pointers, on the headquarters staff. They were there to provide expertise from infantry, artillery, armored, and other branches of the military that would be needed to plan and carry out convincing deceptions.

Three of the four units that made up the Ghost Army reported to Colonel Reeder at Camp Forrest, Tennessee, while the sonic deception unit was organized and trained at the Army Experimental Station, located at Pine Camp in upstate New York. A huge amount of work had to be undertaken in a short time to prepare the various branches of the Ghost Army for action in Europe—not only in the two army camps but also in factories, labs, and testing facilities across the country.

(left) Ellsworth Kelly and an improvised dummy jeep

(right) Soldiers in the 603rd assembling an improvised wooden dummy

The Twenty-Third's largest unit, the 603rd Camouflage Engineers, arrived at Camp Forrest in late January 1944. They did not yet have decoys to work with, so they improvised, fabricating dummy tanks out of wood and burlap and learning how to use them to create convincing deceptions that would fool enemy air reconnaissance. They used a spotter plane to evaluate what they had created and learn how to make things more realistic.

Meanwhile, a mad dash was underway to produce dummies. After conducting tests in the California desert, the army had settled on using

Making Dummy Land Mines
and *Paint Spray Equipment* by
George Vander Sluis, 1943

inflatables. Many of them were designed by Fred Patten, development director of the U.S. Rubber Company plant in Woonsocket, Rhode Island. Patten had also designed the inflatable one-man life rafts carried by fighter pilots in the Pacific.

The tanks were manufactured by a consortium, including U.S. Rubber and other giants such as Goodyear Tire & Rubber Company as well as a collection of smaller companies, such as the L. R. Moulton Drapery Company in Melrose, Massachusetts, the Karl F. Jackson plant in Lowell, Massachusetts, and the Scranton Lace Curtain Manufacturing Company, in Scranton, Pennsylvania.

The first page of a United States Army "Catalog of Targets" listing the variety of dummies available for deception use during World War II, with details on weight and how many would fit into a truck

						SECRET							Sheet 1

CATALOG OF TARGETS — PNEUMATIC —

*Number of uncrated items per Truck, 2½-ton, 6×6, Cargo, L.W.B.

C. of E. Model	Nomenclature	Weight, Lbs.		Bulk, Cu. Ft.		*No. per 2½-T. TK.	Erection		Demounting		Unit Equipment		
		Package	Crated	Package	Crated		Men	Min.	Men	Min.	Trng.	Opnl.	Maint.
1	Car, Half-track, M2	65	160	12	15	26	3	5	3	7	107	375	165
2	Car, 4×4, Scout, M3A1	87	182	12	15	26	3	5	3	7	0	0	0
3	Tank, Light, M5	68	166	13	16	24	3	5	3	7	20	72	30
4	Tank, Medium, M4	73	185	16	20	20	3	5	3	7	42	150	63
5	Trailer, 1-Ton, 2W, Cargo	34	94	6	8	52	3	3	3	5	325	1125	480
6	Truck, ¼-Ton, 4×4	38	103	7	9	45	3	3	3	5	190	563	282
7	Truck, ¾-Ton, Weapons Carrier w/canvas top	58	141	10	13	31	3	5	3	7	73	250	110
7 X	Truck, ¾-Ton Weapons Carrier w/o canvas top	46	111	7	9	45	3	5	3	7	72	250	110
8	Truck, 2½-Ton, 6×6, Cargo, L.W.B. w/canvas top	86	201	18	22	17	3	7	3	10	165	588	250
8 X	Truck, 2½-Ton, 6×6 Cargo, L.W.B w/o canvas top	79	189	17	20	18	3	5	3	7	165	588	250

SECRET

Theresa Ricard's security badge at U.S. Rubber

Jan. 1944

THERESA RICARD

U.S. Rubber temporarily shut down its work on barrage balloons and set up special annexes outside its giant Alice Mill building in Woonsocket in order to meet the deadline for getting the dummies to the Ghost Army. According to a company newsletter written at war's end, "Speed was so essential that men and women were hired on Friday, the locations selected there were renovated Saturday and Sunday, and the decoy work was started the following Tuesday." With the men headed off to war, it was mostly women who picked up the tools to get the job done. Newspaper ads invited women age sixteen to fifty to "help win the war" by working for the rubber company. One of those answering the call was a sixteen-year-old high school student named Theresa Ricard, who ended up gluing together dummy tanks after school for

Barrage balloon, one of thousands manufactured by U.S. Rubber. These held aloft heavy cables used to keep enemy planes from attacking at low altitude.

forty-nine cents an hour. "It stunk. And so did your clothes. When you come out of there, you strip, throw 'em in the washer." She and other workers were told they were making targets. They had no idea until decades later that the dummies were used for quite a different purpose.

The tanks were not simply giant balloons. They were built on a skeleton of inflatable rubber tubes, covered by rubberized canvas. This made them quicker to inflate and also insured that a single piece of shrapnel could not instantly deflate the entire tank. Ricard's job was to work on the tubes that went into the turret. "We'd cement them and fold them different ways to make sure [they would] fit in the turret. We made sure one was long for the gun."

Tanks were not the only inflatables constructed for the Ghost Army. Reporter Fred W. Dudley of the *Lowell Sun* later wrote that entering the Jackson plant in Lowell was like "walking into a fairyland as one sees jeeps, half tracks, three quarter ton trucks…and innumerable other parts rising magically from heaps of rubbish-appearing material scattered about the floor." Because of the time crunch, the men of the 603rd would not get to work with any of the dummies before they arrived in England. Until then, they had to carry out their training missions with handmade substitutes.

The unit selected for radio deception was the 244th Signal Company, commanded by Captain Irwin C. Vander Heide, who had been the chief switchman at the telephone office in Santa Monica, California. Unlike the 603rd, however, this unit did not join the Ghost Army intact.

(top) Inflatable half-track and artillery piece on the factory floor

(bottom) Improvised dummy artillery piece

Stanley Nance and the jeep he named Kilowatt Kommand

To handle the myriad challenges of radio deception, 40 percent of the unit was weeded out and replaced with more than one hundred skilled radio operators plucked from units around the country. The unit was renamed the Signal Company Special.

One of those chosen was Sergeant Stanley Nance, a highly skilled telegrapher. Nance was a ukulele player and had learned strumming techniques that he transferred to the telegraph, giving him lightning-fast speed as an operator. He was on desert maneuvers with the Eleventh Armored Division when a stranger in a jeep came looking for him. "He said, 'Get your equipment and come with me.' And I said, 'Where are you going?' and he said, 'All I can tell you is I'm not supposed to tell you anything, and for you to shut up.'" Lieutenant Bob Conrad, a signal officer for the Thirty-First Infantry Division, was another who found himself suddenly transferred to a mysterious new unit. He had no idea why he was there or what he was supposed to do, so he questioned a senior officer. That's when he first learned about the dangerous aspects of serving in a unit designed to attract enemy attention, likely to be followed shortly by enemy fire. "He said: 'Let's put it this way, Lieutenant. If we are totally successful, you may not come back.'"

Sergeant Spike Berry, a college freshman who had worked part-time at a radio station in Minnesota, considered radio the stage setter. "When you think of the Twenty-Third Special Troops, you think of the inflatable tanks or the sound guys, and they're great. But they have to have a stage on which to perform. And we provided that stage."

German intelligence was highly dependent on radio interception to indicate what the enemy was doing. In North Africa the British had captured an entire German radio interception unit. Military historian Jonathan Gawne says they were stunned to learn how precisely the Germans could pinpoint where a unit was located by analyzing its radio traffic. By later estimates, German army units gathered as much as 75 percent of their intelligence from radio intercepts.

Ghost Army officers carefully studied the pattern of radio transmissions broadcast by the unit they were assigned to impersonate. Lieutenant Bob Conrad and other officers would "meet with the unit's chief signal officer to learn specific call signs, techniques, et cetera practiced by that division." That way, if they were simulating an infantry division moving across a given area, they would know how many times regimental headquarters would be likely to send messages to battalion headquarters, for example. They used this information to create realistic radio-deception scenarios. "It's an art of knowing just how many and what type of messages to send," says Gawne. Ghost Army radio operators would handle some of the division's real radio traffic before the deception began, then keep operating as the real unit moved away, lending an extra degree of realism to their deception.

Much of the radio traffic took place via Morse code; the Germans were able to identify an individual operator by his style, or "fist," as it was called. "When sending in code, an individual's way of tapping his dots and dashes can be distinguished as clearly as his handwriting," wrote Ralph Ingersoll, the Special Plans officer who helped coordinate the unit's operations. So Ghost Army radio operators had to become mimics. The signal company trained its radio men to copy the precise techniques of the operators they were imitating, so that as the real radios went off the air and the fake ones took over, nobody would know the difference. "They came schooled in the styles and accents of every division due to be on the line," wrote Ingersoll. "They had inventories of every real operator's nicknames and peculiarities." Stanley Nance recalled that he would study a radio operator for hours to learn his idiosyncrasies. To this day some experts claim that copying another operator's fist is almost impossible. The fact is, however, that the Twenty-Third's high-speed telegraphers did it routinely.

In early January 1944 the commander of the 293rd Engineer Combat Battalion, taking part in desert maneuvers in Yuma, Arizona, received an order to detach his best company for a secret mission. He selected Company A, a crack unit commanded by recent West Point graduate Lieutenant George Rebh. Rebh was promoted to captain, and his unit became the 406th Engineer Combat Company Special.

Officers of the 406th: from left, Lieutenant William Aliapoulos, Lieutenant John Kelper, Captain George Rebh, Lieutenant Thomas Robinson, and Lieutenant George Daley

The soldiers in the 406th had undergone two years of combat training, and Rebh thought their mission would likely involve demolition work in support of an infantry attack, a prospect that he looked forward to. "Being a regular army officer, you go to the sound of where the guns are firing." He was disappointed to find out that was not the case, although he later came to believe that being in the Ghost Army was extremely beneficial to his army career.

The 406th would act as the unit's security force—to be, as one of the men put it, "the only real soldiers in the unit." At Camp Forrest they

Captain Douglas
Fairbanks Jr.

focused on physical fitness and combat training. As it turned out, once they were in the field they would find a role in the deception mission as well.

Nearly one thousand miles northeast of Camp Forrest, the sonic deception unit was formed and trained at the Army Experimental Station in upstate New York at Pine Camp (now Fort Drum). Using recorded sound to fool the enemy was a new strategy in World War II, made possible by technology that didn't exist a few years earlier.

The military started experimenting with sonic deception in 1942. The United States Navy was the first to make operational use of the idea, thanks to actor-turned-naval-officer Douglas Fairbanks Jr. After observing British Commandos operations, Fairbanks was eager to form a navy deception team. The result was the Beach Jumpers program: small boats equipped with speakers and smoke machines used to create diversions during beach landings. Formed in 1943, the Beach Jumpers saw action in Italy.

The army followed suit, setting up its own sonic deception program under a colorful and charismatic officer named Hilton Howell Railey. Growing up in New Orleans, Railey had dreamed of becoming an actor but instead turned to journalism. After serving in the army during World War I, he went to Poland as a war correspondent. In the 1920s he helped organize Admiral Richard E. Byrd's Antarctic expeditions and recruited Amelia Earhart to fly across the Atlantic—launching her to international fame. When *Fortune* magazine dispatched him to investigate the European arms industry, a Nazi agent tried (without success) to recruit him as Hitler's PR man in America. In the late 1930s he wrote articles on military preparedness and penned a popular autobiography, *Touched with Madness*. A book reviewer for the *New York Times* wrote, "The author shows conclusively that he is again ready and capable of meeting fate on its own ground." World War II would give him a chance.

His first job was to write a confidential report for the army on how to combat low morale among draftees. This led directly to the *Why We Fight* films, directed by Frank Capra, which explained to soldiers the reasons for America's involvement in the war and the principles they were fighting for. Railey was then recalled to service as a colonel and put to work on sonic deception. Headstrong and debonair, he was the perfect person to handle the job. "He had style. He had grace," recalled Lieutenant Dick Syracuse. "This guy was certainly a leader." At Pine Camp, Railey went to work training two sonic units. The 3132 Signal Service Company Special served in the Ghost Army, while the 3133 operated independently in Italy.

Railey personally interviewed many of the officers chosen for the 3132, including Syracuse—a Bronx native who had been commanding an all-black chemical-warfare company training in the South. After he demanded equal privileges for his men, Syracuse suddenly found himself transferred and put on a train back north. He and Railey hit it off immediately. "I can remember so well his greeting to me was, 'Lieutenant, the mission of your company will be to draw enemy fire.' I suggested that as a kid from the Bronx, I certainly respect the role we have to play, but I reserve the right to kick a little ass myself if I get the opportunity. And he roared. He said, 'I love it.'"

Another one who made the cut was Sergeant Jack McGlynn of Medford, Massachusetts. "I was interviewed for a top-secret organization, which was involved in psychological warfare and something to do with sound. I thought: sound—we were going to zap all the Germans; we'd end the war and that would be it. But it was more psychology than zapping."

Members of the Sonic Company Special. Colonel Hilton Howell Railey is front row center, and Sergeant Jack McGlynn is third from the left in the back row.

Their mission was to simulate the sounds of troop movement and activity, especially at night, when enemy observation posts could hear but not see. The army considered using commercially available sound-effects recordings but decided that they would not offer adequate variety. An army report noted that trained observers could differentiate among types of tanks by the sound that they made, and could also determine a tank's speed and whether it was going uphill or downhill. All these different sounds, and many more, needed to be recorded for use in different scenarios.

In early 1944 Railey sent a team with a portable audio studio down to the army proving ground at Fort Knox, Kentucky. An armored company of eighteen Sherman tanks and two hundred men rumbled around the maneuver grounds for three weeks to create the sound effects they would need. The area was closed off to all other activity, and planes were banned from flying over.

Ghost Army technicians worked side by side with experts from Bell Laboratories to record the sounds. A microphone with a burlap windscreen was set up on a tripod. In a van one hundred feet away, two soldiers manned turntables on which a recording head etched grooves into sixteen-inch transcription disks, the same kind used to make hit records. They captured the sounds of tanks, trucks, bulldozers, even the assembly of pontoon bridges used to ford rivers. "You could hear 'em hammering away and swearing," marveled Private Harold Flinn. The Bell Labs engineers developed new techniques for recording sounds for deception purposes. For example, if a truck races past a microphone, the pitch of the sound will drop, due to a scientific principle known as the Doppler effect. That could be a dead giveaway to an enemy

Uncovering the speakers on a sonic half-track

Mobile weather station

observer, since that effect would not normally be heard from far away. To avoid this telltale change in pitch, they came up with the clever idea of locating a microphone at the center of a circle of continuously moving vehicles, so that sounds were recorded free of the Doppler effect.

Various sounds could be cued up on different turntables and mixed together to create whatever scenario was required—one of the earliest known uses of multitrack recording. These mixes were then recorded on a wire recorder—a predecessor to the tape recorder that was advanced technology in the early 1940s. A single spool contained two miles of magnetized wire, enough for thirty minutes of sound; unlike a record, it would never skip.

The recordings were played over five-hundred-pound speakers mounted on half-tracks. On the back of his half-track, recalled Corporal Al Albrecht, "was the biggest boom box you ever saw. But it played sounds of tanks and activity." To evaluate different speaker systems, the Army turned to Harvard University's Electro-Acoustic Laboratory, run by a young scientist named Leo Beranek. "Because of the intense sound levels that such powerful systems had to produce," wrote Beranek, "they could not conveniently be tested outdoors." Instead, Beranek built a sound-deadening chamber that would hide the testing from the public. The result became known as Beranek's Box. It was a room with no echo at all, one of the first ever constructed. Beranek even coined a new word to describe it, calling it an "anechoic" chamber. The forty-by-fifty-foot room, nearly four stories in height, was lined with nineteen thousand fiberglass wedges—nine boxcars' worth. "This meant that you had a room that was almost perfectly quiet. You couldn't hear any noise from outside, and you could hear the blood rushing in your ear, which was a new experience." Beranek eventually became one of the founders of the legendary high-tech company Bolt, Beranek and Newman (now BBN Technologies), which did much of the early engineering work on the Internet. Over the years, thousands of anechoic chambers have been built for audio testing, most using the wedge design pioneered by Beranek and inspired by the Ghost Army.

No detail was overlooked. Wind speed and direction had to be factored in to each deception, so the army created a mobile weather

Leo Beranek (right) in the anechoic chamber that became known as Beranek's Box

station to go into action with the sonic unit. Bell Labs put together firing tables—charts similar to those used by the artillery—to determine how loud to project the sound, depending on the weather, the terrain, and the distance of the enemy.

The result of all this technology and effort was remarkable. Clare Beck, an officer who worked with Harris and Ingersoll in the Special Plans branch in London, returned to the United States to assess the development of sonic deception and came away impressed. "The sonic equipment I observed is excellent and practical," he wrote in his report. "The max range is 7000 yards for motor convoy sounds and bridge building activities, and approximately four thousand yards for sounds of tanks. The sound is projected with deceptive fidelity, and in my opinion and the opinion of others is so near like the real sound as to be impossible to distinguish from it."

Of course, any technology is only as good as the men who operate it, and Railey felt he was sending to Europe a team of the very best, as he expressed in a letter to the father of Sergeant John Borders. "John is a member of a pioneer unit which is unique in the Army of the United States. Never anywhere in my command experience—in three wars— have I known finer men. I claim them for my very own."

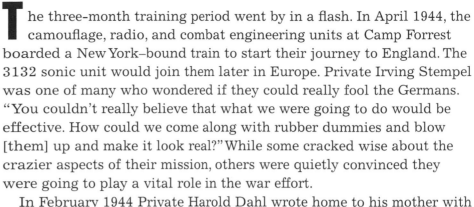

The three-month training period went by in a flash. In April 1944, the camouflage, radio, and combat engineering units at Camp Forrest boarded a New York–bound train to start their journey to England. The 3132 sonic unit would join them later in Europe. Private Irving Stempel was one of many who wondered if they could really fool the Germans. "You couldn't really believe that what we were going to do would be effective. How could we come along with rubber dummies and blow [them] up and make it look real?" While some cracked wise about the crazier aspects of their mission, others were quietly convinced they were going to play a vital role in the war effort.

In February 1944 Private Harold Dahl wrote home to his mother with a hint about their secret mission and where it might take them. "We have a special job to do and it can't be done in our own back yard so we have to play in someone else's." Shortly before leaving Camp Forrest, Dahl wrote again to his sister Lucy in Towaco, New Jersey, emphasizing the need to keep quiet about what he was doing:

Free doughnuts for the departing troops

> See to it, even if you have to explain it to whoever
> reports news from Towaco, that nothing gets in the paper
> if and when we leave. And you & Mother & the others must
> take it as part of your burden not to so much as tell
> anyone that I have gone until we get there and mail comes
> back to you. And then, if you get an idea where I am, don't
> tell anyone, no matter who. This thing we are doing might
> be suspected if it gets out that the 603rd is gone - we
> must be simply forgotten - until after our job is done. It
> really can be terribly important in the war and we have to
> be more than ordinarily careful. I'm sure you understand.

Sergeant Victor Dowd, another member of the camouflage unit, took a different attitude as the journey to the war zone began. He and some of his platoon had a hard time taking the whole thing seriously—at least for the moment. "We didn't really believe the big picture," recalled Dowd. "Until we got fired at and shot. When reality struck."

(opposite) *Military Transport* by Joseph Mack

On board the USNS *Henry Gibbins*, from Victor Dowd's 1944 sketchbook

JOURNEY INTO THE UNKNOWN

All of a sudden I see four guys, one on each
end of a General Sherman tank, picking the thing up.
And I practically collapsed, because I thought,
"Gee, I could never pick up a tank."

— Private Joe Spence

Most of the Ghost Army (not including the sonic unit) sailed from New York to England on May 2, 1944, aboard the USNS *Henry Gibbins*. It was "one of the biggest convoys you could imagine," according to Sergeant Bob Tompkins. "You [saw] ships all the way to the horizon on either side." The men occupied themselves with nightly music and comedy shows, boxing matches, and endless craps games.

They arrived in Bristol, England, on May 15.

From there they traveled to stately Walton Hall, near Stratford-upon-Avon, where they would bivouac. The lush grounds included velvet lawns, tailored forests, and a swan lake. The enlisted men camped out in huts and tents, while the officers had more comfortable quarters inside Walton Hall, sometimes referred to as "Mouldy Manor."

Some men attended the superb plays staged by the
Shakespeare Memorial Theatre in Stratford-on-Avon,
but most seemed to prefer the more realistic pleasures
of Leamington Spa.
— Official History of the 23rd Headquarters Special Troops

They readied themselves for their part in the upcoming invasion. The equipment—from dummies to radios—had arrived before them and had to be gathered from warehouses throughout southern England. Finally, the men of the 603rd had a chance to work with the equipment they would be taking to France. The mission suddenly seemed far more real than it had back in the States. "We knew we would now be really using this stuff," recalled Corporal Jack Masey. "It was thrilling."

Walton Hall

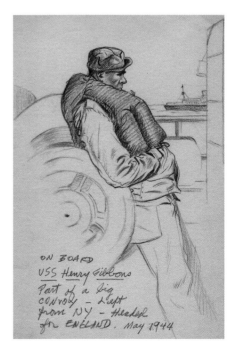

(top) *Convoy* by Richard Morton, 1944

(bottom left) *Soldier in Life Jacket* by Ellsworth Kelly, 1944

(bottom right) On board the USNS *Henry Gibbins*, from Victor Dowd's 1944 sketchbook

(top) *Gunner Onboard* by
Victor Dowd, 1944

(bottom) *Convoy* by Arthur
Singer, 1944

Inflating Tank at Night by
Arthur Shilstone, 1985

Private Joe Spence was a late addition to the camouflage battalion, joining it in England. He knew nothing about the deception mission. His first hint that this was going to be something out of the ordinary came when he arrived at Walton Hall and found it surrounded by a regiment of British paratroopers. The next shock came when "all of a sudden I see four guys, one on each end of a General Sherman tank, picking the thing up. And I practically collapsed, because I thought: 'Gee, I could never pick up a tank.'"

The dummies came in oversized canvas duffels. "It was a little bundle of stuff, which a tank was in," said Jack Masey. The soldiers would open the bundle, spread it out, and inflate the tank through multiple nozzles. "[We would pull out] this amorphic shape," remarked Private Ned Harris, "and then [watch] it being filled with air and taking form like a monster." It took fifteen to twenty minutes to inflate a single tank. "And we all had a very grand time doing it," recalled Masey, "joking and laughing as these things took shape."

From May 29 to June 3 they carried out three practice deceptions called Cabbage, Cheese, and SPAM in the Thetford Maneuver Area, about 110 miles east of Walton Hall. Roy Eichhorn, former director of research and development at the United States Army Combined Arms Center, points out that this is the same part of England where

Operation Fortitude, the D-Day deception, was in full swing at the time. The goal of Fortitude was to convince the Germans that General George Patton was assembling an army that would land at the Pas-de-Calais, more than two hundred miles up the coast from Normandy. Eichhorn believes that the Ghost Army maneuvers may have been planned there to help enhance the D-Day deception.

Once back at Walton Hall, the men of the Twenty-Third checked and rechecked their equipment, went on long training hikes, and let off steam at local pubs. The 406th Combat Engineers offered classes in demolition. On June 5 they heard the drone of airplanes all night long. "In the morning the sky was filled with airplanes headed to France," recalled Private First Class William Anderson. "We knew this was D-Day." A few days later, some of the men in the 406th heard the sounds of a bridge

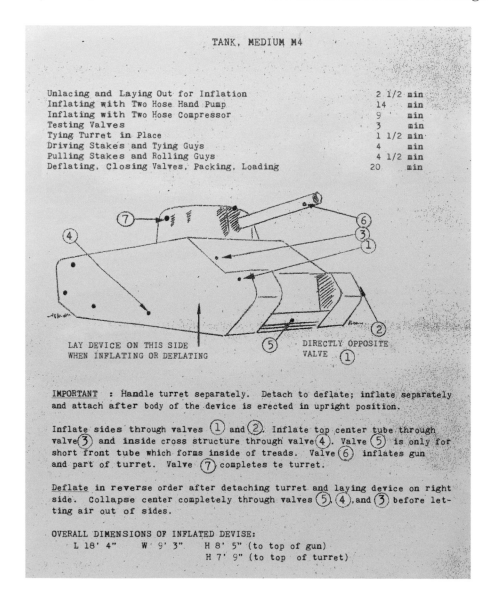

Diagram for inflating M4 dummy tank

Bristol, UK by William
Sayles, 1944

being built near their camp. When they went to investigate, they found
a half-track with a speaker mounted on top. The sonic unit had arrived.

Mostly they spent their time waiting. Waiting to head to France.
Waiting for the moment when it would be their turn to "meet the elephant" (the colorful Civil War phrase that alluded to entering combat
for the first time). Waiting, anxiously waiting, to see how their carefully
laid deception plans would work on the killing fields of Europe.

US
0

BROOKLYN 3411

ROME 1562

ST. LOUIS 4621½

ODENTON 3638

LONDON

TULLAHOMA 4211

BERLIN 763

TOKYO 11957

Dummy sign created by some of the GIs while bivouacked in England

5

WHEN FIRST WE PRACTICE TO DECEIVE

You have to see into the mind of your adversary. You have to create for him a misleading picture of the operation to come. And you have to sell it to him with confidence.

— General Wesley Clark, United States Army

A week after the invasion of D-Day I was with this nice girl, and I remember thinking: "What in the hell am I doing in the British countryside with a pretty girl, when there are guys my age being shot at and killed in Normandy?" And I remember kissing her goodnight and riding my bike back to our tent. And there was a light on in our tent, and somebody said, "Who's there?" I said, "Sergeant Dowd," and a voice said, "You better get in here." And I said, "Let me park my bike." And one of the wise-guy members of the platoon said, "You're not going to need your bike anymore." The next day we were on Omaha Beach in Normandy.

— Sergeant Victor Dowd

On June 6, 1944, the long-awaited Allied invasion exploded onto the beaches of Normandy. More than 150,000 soldiers stormed ashore from an armada of landing craft or parachuted from waves of airplanes overhead. In the days that followed, tens of thousands more followed them across the English Channel, expanding the beachhead and moving slowly into Hitler's Fortress Europe. As the Ghost Army waited its turn, surprise orders came down for a fifteen-man platoon from the 603rd to head to Normandy with dummy artillery ahead of most of the rest of the unit. (A handful of radiomen went in on the morning after D-Day for a mission that was eventually aborted.) It was an experiment of sorts, designed to see if they could really fool the Germans and survive.

The Fourth Platoon of Company D was commanded by Bernie Mason, a twenty-four-year-old lieutenant from Philadelphia. Mason was a high school graduate, with a flair for design, who had gone through Officer Candidate School and ended up in the 603rd. On June 13 he was drinking flag-wavers at a British pub when he got a message ordering him to report back to base immediately. A flag-waver, according to Mason, was a drink so named because it was composed of red amaretto and white gin, "and if you had enough of them you would be blue in the morning."

Mason and his men, including Victor Dowd, were issued ammunition, and they loaded their dummies onto a C-47 cargo plane. Mason still had a hangover when they took off the following morning for Normandy. Dowd was surprised

Bernie Mason by Victor Dowd

American troops
disembarking on Omaha
Beach, Normandy

to find that some of their fellow passengers were women. He asked
what they were doing there. They told him they were nurses and that
after the plane offloaded its cargo, they would be caring for the severely
wounded men who were going to be loaded aboard and rushed back
to England. It was a chilling foretaste of the scene that awaited them
in France.

They all found it a shock to be plunged so suddenly into a war zone.
The plane landed on a metal mesh runway that engineers had just
built behind Omaha Beach. Litters of wounded men waited alongside
the runway, and the sounds of machine gun fire could be heard in the
distance. One of the first things they saw was a sign that said "Beware
of Mines." Dowd was struck by "the wild difference between last night,
when I was in the lovely, quiet, serene countryside, and the grim reality

Sketch by Victor Dowd

of today." The bodies of many German soldiers lay unburied nearby. Dowd and Mason both gawked at a cow impaled upside down in a tree, more than thirty feet in the air, thrown there by the violence of an explosion. Private Irving Stempel leaned against a wheel of the airplane and dashed off a note to his family, letting them know he had made it safely into Europe. He gave it to the pilot to mail.

Their first night ashore, they huddled in foxholes as an artillery barrage rained down on them. The only one not terrified by the bombardment was Dowd, who somehow managed to sleep through the whole thing. In a spare moment during those first days, he made a sketch of a German "potato-masher" hand grenade and helmet still lying on the ground.

The assignment of "Task Force Mason" was to assist the 980th Artillery, the first heavy-artillery battalion to land in France. It was operating near the town of Sainte-Mère-Église. They set up dummy artillery emplacements about a mile ahead of its position, in order to draw fire away from the real battery. "It was kind of scary," recalled Mason. They found their dummy 155mm howitzers heavy and cumbersome to deal with. After inflating the dummy guns, they covered them with camouflage netting in such a way that they would be enticingly visible to enemy aircraft. Mason's platoon was accompanied by four men from the 406th Combat Engineers, who set off improvised flash canisters to make it look like the firing was coming from their dummies.

Security was obviously critical. The soldiers guarded the perimeter, and people could only get into their emplacement through a narrow entrance. One day a photographer from *Life* showed up looking for a story. He couldn't understand why they wouldn't let him in to photograph what he obviously believed was real artillery and went

Dummy 155mm artillery piece under camouflage netting

away angry. It was not the last time that they would find themselves deceiving their fellow Americans.

For twenty-eight days they followed the real 980th as it moved up into the Cherbourg Peninsula. The experiment proved a success. The Germans shelled their phony guns on multiple occasions, but the Ghost Army managed to avoid suffering any casualties. During one move Lieutenant Mason's jeep ended up behind a truck that in the twilight appeared to be carrying a mass of jelly that jiggled with every bump. "And it turned out that they were the bodies of dead German soldiers. And the odor was so horrific that you can't imagine."

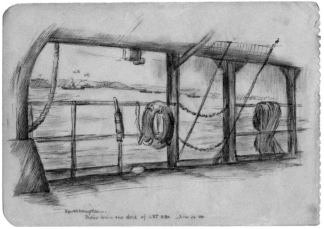

A sketchbook series by Ned Harris, drawn while waiting to cross the channel to Normandy, June 23–26, 1944

The remainder of the Twenty-Third (minus the sonic company, still training in England) came to France in two groups. The first, code-named Elephant, arrived in late June. The second, known as Residue (nicknamed "Garbage" by the men), came in early July. Aboard the landing ship, tank (LST) that would take them across the Channel, they waited day after monotonous day to get underway. "Boredom, and anticipating, and too much time to think," recalled Private Ned Harris. "That's when the sketchbooks come out." Harris made many drawings while they waited, until he finally captured their departure in a vibrant sketch titled *On Our Way*.

The first group anchored off Utah Beach on June 24. The men waited for their names to be called before clambering over the side of the ship and down the cargo nets into the landing boats that would take them to the beach. "We were loaded down with everything," recalled Corporal Arthur Shilstone. "Rifles, ammunition, helmets, and so forth." Despite his heavy load, Shilstone could not resist breaking out his pad and

sketching the incredible scene before him: the vast armada of the invasion force, barrage balloons overhead, and "every imaginable ship as far as you could see." Even in the moment he knew "this was really history in the making."

They bivouacked three miles north of the Normandy village of Trévières. Harris recalls that after making camp, his platoon set up their dummies to make sure they were in working order. A German plane flew overhead that night, strafing American positions. One of the men, caught out of his foxhole, dived under a dummy truck as if it were a real one—much to the amusement of his fellow deceivers. When they awoke the following morning, they were greeted with quite a commotion. A French farmer had come at dawn to check his cows. "And he never saw, in all his years of farming, the sight he saw," said Harris. "His cows were pushing an American tank around his property." The farmer had to be restrained from running into the village to report what he'd witnessed.

(top) *Landing in Normandy* by Arthur Shilstone, 1944

(bottom) Ned Harris's photo of Ghost Army soldiers preparing to climb into landing craft and land on Utah Beach

On another occasion, two Frenchmen on bicycles somehow got through the security perimeter. Shilstone managed to halt them, but not before they had seen more than they should. "What they thought they saw was four GIs picking up a forty-ton Sherman tank and turning it around. They looked at me, and they were looking for answers, and I finally said, 'The Americans are very strong.'"

Such security breaches, humorous as they might be, were no laughing matter. They threatened the success of the mission, yet were difficult to avoid. In their first deception, Operation Elephant, the Twenty-Third took up the positions of the Second Armored Division as the real division moved to a new spot on the line. The mission involved visual and radio deception only, since the sonic unit was still in England. As each unit of the Second Armored moved out, the Twenty-Third attempted to replace real vehicles with dummies—tank for tank, gun for gun. In one farmer's field, a real battery of four antiaircraft guns moved out at night. A few hours later, the dummy guns moved in. The French farmer saw the real guns leaving and was surprised and upset to see new guns in the morning. "*Encore* boom boom?" he complained to the soldiers, angry that there would be more loud firing from so near his house. He brought his fist down on the dummy gun and his hand came bouncing

The Americans Are Very Strong! by Arthur Shilstone, 1985

up. A smile spread across his face. "Boom boom ha ha!" he said. According to Lieutenant Gil Seltzer, that soon became a watchword for the 603rd. (And another French farmer had to be sworn to secrecy.)

But working with dummies wasn't all fun and games. The enemy was never very far away; their presence was keenly felt. It might be a few stray shells from a German 88mm cannon or the occasional strafing by a fighter plane. Corporal John Jarvie felt very vulnerable when he had to go out at one or two in the morning to inflate the dummies and turn on an air compressor that could be heard ten miles away.

General Wesley Clark argues that deception requires the highest form of creativity in the art of war. "You have to see into the mind of your adversary. You have to create for him a misleading picture of the operation to come. And you have to sell it to him with confidence." Operation Elephant was, in essence, the Twenty-Third's shakedown cruise, a chance to see if they could live up to that dictum. The operation was plagued with problems, including late orders, misunderstandings, and a lack of coordination with the unit the Twenty-Third was impersonating. But even if it wasn't a rousing success, it offered the men an opportunity to hone their technique. Visual deception, for example, demanded an artist's eye for detail. "We could position things so that they would be hidden, but kind of hidden in plain sight," said

Jarvie. When a reconnaissance plane came over, it might spot just the corner of one dummy, but that would be enough to signal that there were more they couldn't see. Each tableau had to be carefully dressed. A cluster of tanks does not look believable from the air unless each vehicle has tracks leading up to it. So the men of the 406th Combat Engineers took turns operating a bulldozer to fill the fields with simulated tank tracks. If a dummy artillery piece was set up, it had to have empty shells strewn around it, just as a real one would.

These lessons would come in handy for future operations. There was lots of room for improvement. A few days after Elephant was concluded, Lieutenant Fred Fox wrote a memo that eventually went out to the men of the unit under the name of Colonel Harry L. Reeder, the unit's commander. It read, in part:

```
The attitude of the Twenty-third HQs towards their mission
is lopsided. There is too much MILITARY and not enough
SHOWMANSHIP.
   Like it or not, the Twenty-third HQ must consider
itself a traveling road show ready at a moment's notice to
present:
   THE SECOND ARMORED DIVISION - by Brooks
   THE NINTH INFANTRY DIVISION - by Eddy
   THE SEVENTH CORPS - by Collins
   The presentations must be done with the greatest accuracy
and attention to detail. They will include the proper
scenery, props, costumes, principals, extras, dialogue,
and sound effects. We must remember that we are playing
to a very critical and attentive radio, ground, and aerial
audience. They must all be convinced.
```

After Elephant, the soldiers spent much of July waiting for the opportunity to put into use what they had learned. The men used the time to explore their new surroundings. Artists in the unit broke out their paints and pencils. "Any given opportunity, guys would draw," said John Jarvie. "Guys would draw with a fountain pen and spit. You make the drawing, and you wet it, and it makes nice halftones." Arthur Shilstone was another who felt the urge. "To be in the middle of this incredible adventure," he said, "with a world at war, in a foreign country? I just had to put it down."

They sketched and painted on whatever was handy: a notebook, an index card, an old receipt. They drew each other, French families, and bombed-out farmhouses. "We were sleeping in hedgerows and foxholes," said Jarvie, "but nothing kept us away from going someplace to do a watercolor."

Calvados, a powerful native stimulant, was sampled. Private contracts for laundry were made with local farmwomen who preferred candy, soap and cigarettes to francs. Towns were OFF LIMITS but some visiting was done on various pretexts. One scheme that worked for a long time was to tell the MPs you were looking for blue paint. No Army supply dump carried this color.

— Official History of the 23rd Headquarters Special Troops

(top) *German Defense Against Glider Invasion* by Arthur Shilstone, 1944. These logs, called "Rommel's asparagus," were planted by the Germans to prevent American gliders from landing safely.

(bottom) *Normandy '44* by Bill Sayles. This sketch depicts the town of Trévières.

Private Irving Mayer's photo of homeless refugees

The soldiers also observed the miseries of war. "Poor people," wrote Private Harold Dahl to his mother. "Imagine how you would feel if you suddenly found yourself with nothing in the world but a few blankets on a wheelbarrow and all your neighbors in the same boat."

After seven weeks of difficult hedgerow fighting, the First Army punched a hole through German defenses in late July; Operation Cobra gave the Allies the breakthrough they had been fighting for. General Omar Bradley, commander of the Twelfth Army Group, activated General George Patton's Third Army.

On August 9, 1944, Captain Ralph Ingersoll found himself in a jeep headed to a meeting with "Old Blood and Guts," as the press had nicknamed Patton. The Twenty-Third had been given a new mission: Operation Brittany. They were to give the impression that the Americans were weakening their forces in front of the main battle position and turning west to clear the Brittany peninsula, when in fact General Patton was being unleashed to race east and surround the Germans.

Ingersoll, as one of the officers coordinating Ghost Army deceptions, was delegated to let Patton know what was going on. He found the general's command trailer in an apple orchard. Patton was resplendent as ever, complete with ivory-handled pistols, polished boots, and sardonic mien. "I got the message you were coming to save me," he said sarcastically. But then he waved the deception planner to a seat and listened closely, suggesting a change or two to make the plan more realistic. He even promised to detail some fighting troops to provide security for the deceivers.

"It was just then," wrote Ingersoll years later in an unpublished memoir, "with my Top Secret mission accomplished, that I got a front row seat at a non-secret Georgie Patton performance. It was my single personal experience with the fabulous Patton." As Ingersoll looked on, an armored vehicle pulled up and out popped a young American lieutenant colonel. He turned to help another officer climb out: a captive German general being brought to Patton for interrogation. Lieutenant General Karl Spang had been captured near Brest. The American officer was still assisting Spang when Patton unleashed a bellow: "Stop kissing that Kraut bastard's ass! Who do you think he is? Jesus Christ? Kick his goddamn ass over here and kick it fast."

Ingersoll stood with mouth agape. "By this time," he wrote, "the quaking representative of the Third Reich was doing what he could to hold himself at attention. He was pale and visibly shaken (as was I)."

Then, as quickly as Patton had turned his anger on, he turned it off. "Patton's whole personality seemed to change." He shook hands with General Spang, invited him in to the trailer, and had a drink with him. "Sit down and rest a spell," Ingersoll recalls Patton saying. "There's no reason we shouldn't make some comradely conversation before you have to go." Ingersoll decided it was time to beat a hasty retreat.

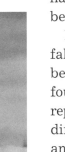

General George Patton

In Army parlance, a "notional" unit is the fake force you are trying to get the enemy to believe in. The Twenty-Third assembled into four task forces slicing into Brittany. Each represented a notional combat team from a different division: the Thirty-Fifth, Eightieth, and Ninetieth Infantry Divisions, and the Second Armored Division. They moved west, away from the main German line and into Brittany. More than seventy inflatable tanks were used, but because they were moving away from where the enemy could see them, radio was a central part of their deception. They set up a powerful radio network that generated a stream of messages back and forth with Third Army Headquarters in the hopes that German signal intelligence officers were listening in.

Military historian Jonathan Gawne believes this might have been one of the Ghost Army's most important deceptions. Operation Brittany may have helped fool the Germans long enough to let Patton's real troops get around behind the German Seventh Army and destroy the main German force in France. This despite the fact that Patton never came through with the infantry he said he would supply for security. Ingersoll got in touch with an officer at Third Army HQ to find out what happened to the promised troops and received this word back: "The General says to tell Ingersoll that his boy scouts would have learned more of what a real war is like if they had been shot at."

In truth, though, despite Patton's reputation and his more than occasional posturing, he could grasp the value of deception far better than most generals in that war. Ingersoll and his boss, Colonel Billy Harris, found Patton easy to work with. "He was the greatest team player that we ran into over there," said Harris. "He would do anything you asked him to do in the interest of the overall picture." Perhaps that's why so many Ghost Army deceptions in the coming months would involve the Third Army.

Letter home from Sergeant
Joseph Mack

My Darling —

the drawing below is my new home I told you about — incomprehensive isn't it + with good reason — I am practically out of paint — but anyway, I guess you get the idea — straw bed — cardboard wall + etc — It rained like all holy hell today + I think I was one of the very few who didn't get wet. If you will notice I left out all G.I. equipment to make sure it goes through the censor, in one of the boxes at the far end of the bunk I have the Kerosene lamp — and I kept it lit all day + it gave the place

— FRENCH CHATEAULET —
(G.I. STYLE)

a more cheerful atmosphere — according to G.I. standards I am living good, however according to civilian standards I am living as a hobo would — (so whats the matter with a hobo's life ?) I've been sleeping most of the day — didn't even go to chow — had a can of salmon + dozens of hard tack (crackers) + if

By mid-August, the Allies had scored a striking victory. Massive German forces had been encircled by American, British, Canadian, and Polish forces that linked up near the Normandy town of Falaise. Ten thousand Germans were killed and another fifty thousand captured in what became known as the Falaise Pocket. The rest were disorganized and on the run. The way to Paris and the German border suddenly seemed wide open for the Allies.

> While the 23rd does not hold itself responsible for the destruction of the German SEVENTH ARMY, there is always a possibility that its ruse helped becloud the German estimate of the situation.
> — Official History of the 23rd Headquarters Special Troops

The deceivers were starting to hit their stride. What's more, during Operation Brittany, the Ghost Army had unveiled a new type of deception that would become an increasingly essential part of their toolkit over the course of the war. This method, born of their experiences on the ground in France, would soon turn every last one of them into full-fledged thespians.

A Church in Trévières

In early July 1944 Ghost Army artists made their way into the Normandy village of Trévières to sketch and paint the bombed-out church off the town square. The village children came and gazed over their shoulders. Some of the children fished out pieces of stained glass from the rubble, which they traded for chocolate. John Jarvie had a stained-glass lamp made with the fragments he brought home.

The church is visible in the upper right corner of the aerial photo. It has since been completely restored, along with the rest of the town.

Phil Hornthal and Edward
Boccia sketching in the church

(opposite) *Trévières Church,
Interior* by Arthur Singer,
1944

(opposite) *Trévières Church, Exterior* by Arthur Singer, 1944

(left) *Paul Gravey* by John Hapgood, 1944, depicts one of the children who traded stained-glass fragments for chocolates.

(right) *Church Steeple*, 1944 by Bob Tompkins

Two GIs stencil fake markings on a jeep.

6

SPECIAL EFFECTS

We were turned loose in town
[and told to] go to the pub, order some omelets,
order some cider, and talk loose.

— John Jarvie

T hree United States Army jeeps roared through the small Luxembourg village, just a few miles from the front lines near the German border. It was early September 1944, three months after D-Day. The vehicles in front and back bristled with guards and machine guns. The one in the middle bore the distinctive red license plate of a major general. In the backseat sat a ramrod figure sporting a magnificent military moustache and general's stars. All three jeeps were clearly identifiable by their markings as belonging to the Sixth Armored Division.

The convoy pulled up to a tavern run by a suspected Nazi collaborator. The general and his bespectacled aide strode inside. With the help of their bodyguards, they liberated six cases of fine wine, loading them onto the general's jeep. The little convoy then took off, leaving the seething proprietor plenty of incentive to get word to the Germans about what he had just witnessed: the American Sixth Armored was moving into what was otherwise a thinly held area.

In fact, the whole bit was a carefully choreographed flimflam. The Sixth Armored was far away. The commanding presence in the back seat was no general but a mustachioed major playing king for a day. The performance he and the other soldiers put on that day was a particularly dramatic example of a deception technique concocted on the ground by the men of the Ghost Army. It became known as "atmosphere" or "special effects."

The Ghost Army came to France prepared to conduct a multimedia show using three kinds of deception: visual, radio, and sonic. Moving through the French villages so recently occupied by the Germans, where spies and collaborators no doubt remained, the men in the unit saw

Café de l'Est by William Sayles, 1944

Fred Fox's ID badge

an opportunity to improvise yet another way of deceiving the enemy, one that hadn't been planned in advance but might pay big dividends. Unlike many ideas in the military, it began with the enlisted men and worked its way upward. Perhaps its strongest advocate was a charismatic young lieutenant (eventually promoted to captain) named Fred Fox.

Fox was a 1939 graduate of Princeton who fancied himself the next Jimmy Stewart (Princeton '32). He went out to Hollywood to seek his fame and fortune but ended up writing baby-food commercials for NBC Radio. After the war broke out he enlisted and eventually ended up in the Ghost Army. Fox found himself right at home in this off-off-Broadway show. "He was very innovative and creative," recalled Sergeant Spike Berry.

Fox's stage training led him to argue passionately for taking a more theatrical approach to their deceptions. If they were portraying the Seventy-Fifth Infantry Division, he reasoned, they should wear Seventy-Fifth Division patches on their uniforms, put Seventy-Fifth markings on their trucks, and drive back and forth through towns. Men should be versed in the details of the Seventy-Fifth so they could talk about it to civilians.

Bob Tompkins (left), Bill Blass (second from right), and buddies at a French cafe

A Small Cognac by Edward Boccia, 1945

There should be a phony headquarters bustling with officers. "Road signs, sentry posts, bumper markings, and the host of small details which betray the presence of a unit should be reconnoitered and duplicated with special teams of the 23rd," he wrote in a memo.

The idea was quickly adopted. "So we began to put on [other divisions'] patches and put their bumper markings on, and we physically assumed the role," said Lieutenant Dick Syracuse, "only for every hundred of them, there might be ten of us." Soldiers wearing the patches of the unit being impersonated would show up at local cafes, spinning their phony stories for whatever spies lurked in the shadows. "We were turned loose in town," remembered Corporal John Jarvie, and told to "go to the pub, order some omelets, order some cider, and talk loose."

"Behind every operation was a touch of Fred Fox," said Berry. Fox took on the role of scriptwriter and director. "Members of the decoy unit were trained to spill phony stories at the local bars and brothels," Fox recalled, "which didn't require much training." Berry remembered that Fox would coach the men before each deception. "He'd get us in a huddle and say, 'This is what's going to happen, and this is what we want you to say, and just be natural.' For example, guys went to the bakery, got some rolls, and said, 'We got to get an extra supply because we're moving out tonight,' that kind of thing."

Roy Eichhorn, former director of research and development at the United States Army Combined Arms Center, whose stepfather, George

A few of the patches the Ghost Army soldiers wore during their "special effects" missions. These are for the Seventy-Fifth, Ninety-Fifth, and Sixty-Ninth Infantry Divisions.

Sewing Patches by Arthur Shilstone, 1985

Martin, served in the unit, says that in some cases the men would layer the phony patches on their uniforms, with the largest on top and the smallest underneath, so they could impersonate multiple units. "OK, we're done being this unit, everybody rip, go into the next town, raise hell and tear up the next bar, and move on." Corporal Jack Masey recalled that his shirts were wrecked because he sewed so many patches onto them.

The men embraced their deceptions with enthusiasm. "We'd find out if a division or a special unit had a particular song that they liked to sing," remembered Syracuse. "We'd get blitzed and then sing their song!" The soldiers in the 406th Combat Engineers became expert at impersonating military policemen (MPs) and frequently operated traffic-control checkpoints that many real units passed through, not realizing they were brushing up against a secret unit. During Operation Brittany, Captain Oscar Seale and Private Charles Gorman hit upon a handy means to carry out their deception. They went into more than a dozen bars in Rennes in the guise of Eightieth Infantry Division MPs. Each time, they announced loudly to any GIs within that the bar was now off limits and ordered them to finish their drinks and scram. Seale and Gorman made sure to have a drink or two in each one, spreading the word of the Eightieth's arrival. By the end of the evening, everybody in town "knew" the Eightieth was moving in.

Fox was adamant that the soldiers in the unit needed to be free to impersonate generals. "Nothing gives away the location of an important unit quicker than a silver-starred jeep," he wrote in a memo. The fact that such an impersonation was a court-martial offense carried no sway with him. "Is not the whole idea of 'impersonation' contrary to (army regulations)?" he wrote. "Remember we are in the theater business. Impersonation is our racket. If we can't do a complete job we might as well give up. You can't portray a woman if bosoms are forbidden." He got himself all wound up arguing in favor of such impersonations to Lieutenant Colonel Clifford Simenson, who let Fox go on and on for quite a while before telling him with a chuckle that the idea had already been approved. Ghost Army lieutenants and captains frequently found themselves impersonating colonels and generals. Fox himself played the general's aide in the operation directed against the tavern keeper who was collaborating with the Nazis. Fox's only fear was that their convoy would run into a real general and they would have to explain themselves.

The men did everything they could to mimic the behavior of the troops they were imitating. "If the division used to send a patrol up to the lines at dawn, the special troops did the same," according to Corporal Sebastian Messina. "If the division was prone to play softball in off-duty moments, softball was the game of the day."

The need for secrecy frequently created odd situations. "Not only did we have to deceive the enemy," said retired Major General George Rebh, who as a captain commanded the 406th Combat Engineers, "but we also had to deceive our own people, so they wouldn't spread the word." They wanted to avoid anything that might inadvertently clue the enemy to the fact that there was a deception unit operating against them.

During one deception, Captain Rebh was impersonating a full colonel in a regimental command post. Two officers who had been a year ahead of him at West Point happened into his phony command post and were shocked to see that this underclassman now outranked him. "Here we are about two years later," said Rebh, "and I'd gone from cadet to full colonel, which is quite unusual." On the way out, the pair stopped and asked his first sergeant how Rebh had become a colonel so fast. The sergeant brushed them off with a remark about being in the right place at the right time, and the two officers left shaking their heads, mystified over Rebh's meteoric rise.

Lieutenant Dick Syracuse recalled an operation during which he ran into an old friend serving in another unit. The man noted the Eighty-Third Infantry Division patch Syracuse was wearing. He remembered that the last time he saw Syracuse he was wearing the insignia of the Fifth Armored Division, and before that, another unit. Syracuse was secretly amused that his friend had stumbled upon evidence of his deception work but needed to come up with an explanation. Lowering his voice, he confided that he was a bit of a screwup, so he kept getting transferred. "You better watch yourself," warned his concerned friend.

Sentry in front of phony command post

"They're liable to bust you down and put a rifle in your hands." Syracuse could only smile.

Sergeant Jack McGlynn found himself in a sticky situation during yet another deception. He was driving a jeep with Ninetieth Infantry Division markings when an MP from the real Ninetieth Division stopped him at a checkpoint. This was around the time of the Battle of the Bulge, when the Germans had unleashed their own secret unit of soldiers dressed in American uniforms, so the MPs were on high alert. They asked McGlynn the password. "I don't know," he said. How about last month's password? "I don't know," McGlynn repeated. "I've never had a password."

The MP was now convinced that he might be on the verge of capturing a spy and making a hero out of himself. Gripping his machine gun, he stared down McGlynn as he rapped out another question. "Where are you from?" "Boston," replied McGlynn. "Boston's a big place. Where?" asked the MP. "Medford," said McGlynn.

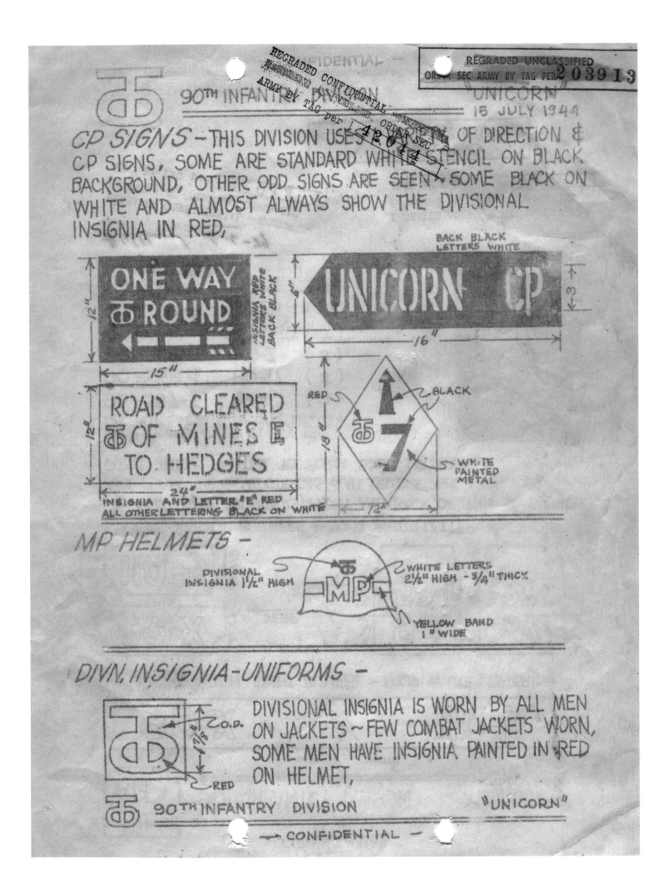

90TH INFANTRY DIVISION "UNICORN"
15 JULY 1944

CP SIGNS - THIS DIVISION USES A VARIETY OF DIRECTION & CP SIGNS, SOME ARE STANDARD WHITE STENCIL ON BLACK BACKGROUND, OTHER ODD SIGNS ARE SEEN, SOME BLACK ON WHITE AND ALMOST ALWAYS SHOW THE DIVISIONAL INSIGNIA IN RED,

ONE WAY 35 ROUND

INSIGNIA RED LETTERS WHITE BACK BLACK

12"
15"

BACK BLACK LETTERS WHITE
UNICORN CP
5"
16"
3"

ROAD CLEARED 35 OF MINES E TO HEDGES
12"
24"
INSIGNIA AND LETTER "E" RED
ALL OTHER LETTERING BLACK ON WHITE

RED
18"
12"
BLACK
WHITE PAINTED METAL

MP HELMETS -

DIVISIONAL INSIGNIA 1½" HIGH
MP
WHITE LETTERS 2½" HIGH - ¾" THICK
YELLOW BAND 1" WIDE

DIVN. INSIGNIA - UNIFORMS -

O.D.
1⅞"
RED

DIVISIONAL INSIGNIA IS WORN BY ALL MEN ON JACKETS ~ FEW COMBAT JACKETS WORN, SOME MEN HAVE INSIGNIA PAINTED IN RED ON HELMET,

90TH INFANTRY DIVISION "UNICORN"

- CONFIDENTIAL -

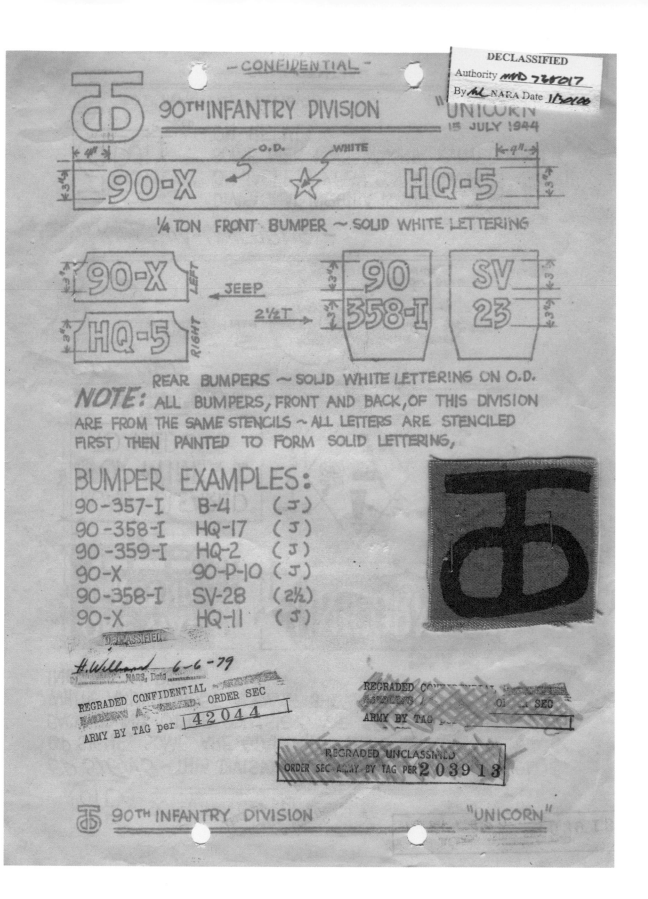

90TH INFANTRY DIVISION "UNICORN"

15 JULY 1944

O.D. WHITE

4" 9"

90-X ☆ HQ-5

¼ TON FRONT BUMPER ~ SOLID WHITE LETTERING

90-X LEFT
HQ-5 RIGHT
← JEEP

90 SV
358-I 23
2½T →

REAR BUMPERS ~ SOLID WHITE LETTERING ON O.D.

NOTE: ALL BUMPERS, FRONT AND BACK, OF THIS DIVISION ARE FROM THE SAME STENCILS ~ ALL LETTERS ARE STENCILED FIRST THEN PAINTED TO FORM SOLID LETTERING.

BUMPER EXAMPLES:

90-357-I	B-4	(J)
90-358-I	HQ-17	(J)
90-359-I	HQ-2	(J)
90-X	90-P-10	(J)
90-358-I	SV-28	(2½)
90-X	HQ-11	(J)

90TH INFANTRY DIVISION "UNICORN"

(opposite and previous)
"Poop sheets" for the
Ninetieth Infantry Division

Then the MP shocked him. "What's the name of the school on Harvard Street?" "The Lincoln School," McGlynn told him, and the MP relaxed. Laughing about the story nearly seventy years later, McGlynn marveled at the lucky coincidence. "Twenty million men and women under arms, and he lived a fifth of a mile from me; I passed his house every day."

In order to prepare for future operations, Ghost Army officers visited the fighting divisions to study their practices. "By V-E Day the Twenty-Third probably contained the most widely traveled and best-informed officers in the ETO," wrote Fox in the unit's official history. Artists in the unit put together what they called "poop sheets" for every division in the Twelfth Army Group, detailing the markings and insignia unique to each. Gathering this information enabled them to carry out an impersonation on a moment's notice. One day Corporal George Martin and another soldier were up on a ladder measuring a sign put up by another division. They were under orders not to reveal to anyone why they were doing so. According to the story Martin told his stepson, Roy Eichhorn, a colonel from that division happened to drive by in a jeep and demanded to know what they were doing.

"Sir," said Martin, in the classic manner of an enlisted man patiently explaining something to a particularly dimwitted superior, "we're measuring this sign."

The colonel, not satisfied with the answer, asked why.

"Well," said Martin, "we've been ordered to measure the signs and make sure they all conform to Army standards."

The colonel exploded. He threw his helmet down on the ground and launched into an epic rant. "Goddamn army! Don't they know there's a war on! Bureaucracy! Idiots! They've got soldiers out measuring signs—don't they know we need soldiers at the front?" The two soldiers ignored him as best they could and went on with their business.

The ultimate purpose of the special effects was to back up the other means of deception and perhaps provide the final confirmation a German intelligence officer might need to believe the phony story put forth by the Ghost Army. "It was almost kind of silly, really," said Private Joe Spence, recalling some of their escapades. "But I think what confirmed the effectiveness was sitting in a cafe and seeing a door open up gradually and somebody taking pictures."

Writing years later, Ralph Ingersoll, the staff officer who helped dream up the unit and oversee its operations, summed up the special-effects tactic this way: "I have no positive evidence that the trick ever worked. But it certainly was worth the playing, and I suspect its cast had the only really enviable job in the whole of World War II."

Laundry by Victor Dowd, 1944

7

"ADOLPH, YOU SON OF A BITCH"

Would give my right arm to sit in front of a cozy fire with my little darling in my arms.

— Diary of Sergeant Bob Tompkins

In mid-August 1944 Allied armies broke out of Normandy and began to sweep across France. The Twenty-Third Headquarters Special Troops were on the move as well. Their destination was the port city of Brest, on the tip of the Brittany peninsula. Brest was under siege by the Allies but still tenaciously held by German paratroopers. The Ghost Army was dispatched to see how they could help in the taking of the city. The trip took two days, and the weather was miserable.

Sergeant Bob Tompkins was a jeep driver in the 603rd and close friends with Private First Class Bill Blass. Tompkins was the younger of the two, but Blass felt that "with his confident manner and dashing good looks, set off by a thin Errol Flynn moustache, he seemed somehow more worldly." Against all security regulations, Tompkins kept a secret diary in a tiny address book. He believed that if he was caught with it, he'd "be shot on the spot." He wrote as small as he could because he was afraid he would run out of space before the fighting was over. After the war Blass's mother typed it up to preserve it for posterity.

Bob Tompkins drew this self-portrait in his jeep's rearview mirror on the way to Brest. "I guess I look pretty miserable, because I was."

August 21, 1944
   Pulled out at 8:10 AM. 158 miles. Drove most of the way with top and windshield down in driving rain. Would give my right arm to sit in front of a cozy fire with my little darling in my arms. Oh Adolph [sic], you son of a Bitch. I feel like a frozen drowned rat.
— Diary of Sergeant Bob Tompkins

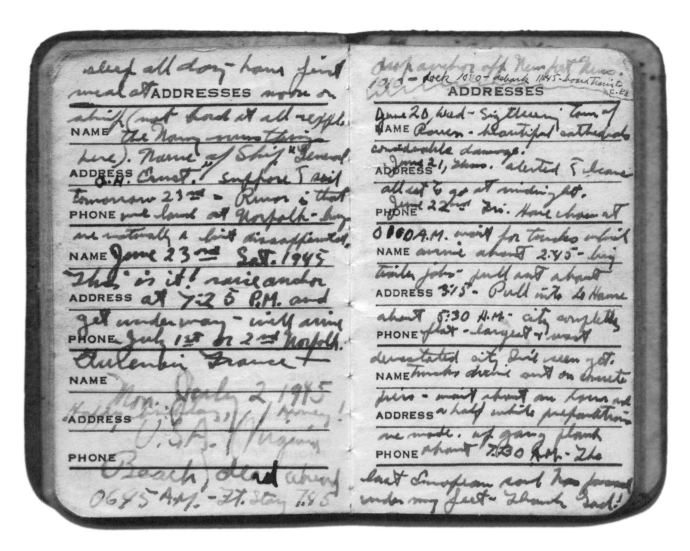

Wartime diary of Bob Tompkins, approximately twice the actual size

Raising the speakers on one of the sonic half-tracks

Three divisions in the American VIII Corps, the Second, Eighth, and Twenty-Ninth, had been assigned the job of taking the city. The mission of the Twenty-Third was to inflate the apparent size of the American forces attacking the city by impersonating the Sixth Armored Division, in the hopes that it would help convince German General Hermann-Bernhard Ramcke to surrender. They were also trying to attract German antitank weapons and reserves to the flanks, to help clear the way for a possible American attack in the center. The sonic unit had just arrived in France, so Operation Brest became the Ghost Army's first chance to use all its means of deception simultaneously.

The unit divided into three notional task forces. Two of them simulated tank battalions. Radio trucks set up along the road to Brest mimicked a convoy pulling in. Sound trucks making their debut underwent a baptism by fire, pulling up to within five hundred yards of German lines to make it seem as if armored

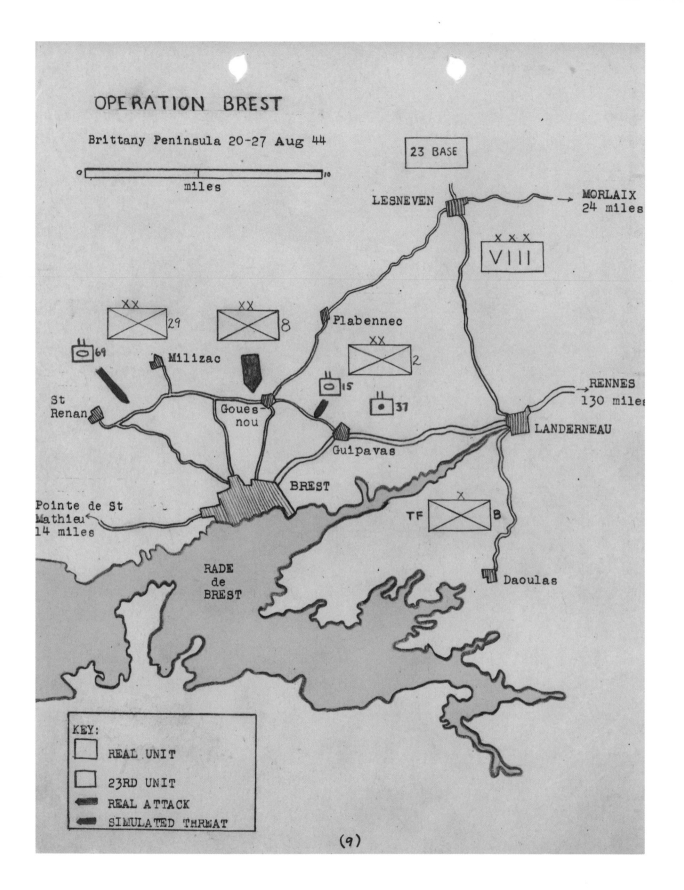

OPERATION BREST

Brittany Peninsula 20-27 Aug 44

0   miles   10

23 BASE

LESNEVEN → MORLAIX 24 miles

XXX
VIII

XX 29

XX 8

Plabennec

69

Milizac

XX 2

Gouesnou

15

37

→ RENNES 130 miles

St Renan

Guipavas

LANDERNEAU

BREST

Pointe de St Mathieu 14 miles

TF   X   B

RADE de BREST

Daoulas

KEY:

REAL UNIT

23RD UNIT

REAL ATTACK

SIMULATED THREAT

(9)

(opposite) Map created in 1945 depicting Operation Brest

units were arriving and making camp. The half-tracks were fitted with explosive charges; the men were under orders to destroy them if it looked as though they were going to be overrun. "There was a glass underneath the dashboard," recalled Private Harold Flinn. "And if you broke that you had so many seconds to get out" before the half-track blew up. Under no circumstances were the sonic vehicles to fall into the hands of the enemy.

A repair shop set up under camouflage netting to patch damaged dummies

More than fifty dummy tanks were set up in the night, along with dummy jeeps and trucks. There was heavy rain, which made the rubber dummies difficult to work with. Camouflage nets were strung up, and the dummy tanks were supplemented with a handful of actual light tanks placed in the most visible positions. The men lit fires, pitched tents, and when they skies cleared they even hung laundry in the area where the fake tanks were set up—all part of the illusion.

August 24, 1944
  Maintained items - tore them down at 9 PM. Moved up 500 yards to new area and set up new tanks. Willy [Blass] and I set up our tent with our feet sticking out in the pouring down rain and passed out around 3 AM.
— Diary of Sergeant Bob Tompkins

Tompkins could see German observers keeping watch from a distant church tower. He and the other men of the 603rd had to keep careful watch on the dummies, especially in the hours before dawn. "During the night, the gun turrets would sag, and that's a bad visual effect the next morning." The men dug in to protect themselves against German shelling, which was commonplace though rarely heavy during the first few days they were there.

Sniper Lookout by Arthur Shilstone, 1944

Special effects were in full swing as well. The men wore the patches of the Sixth Armored Division and put Sixth Armored markings on their trucks, which they drove back and forth between town and their phony tank battalion. GIs from other units who heard the sounds of tanks moving in during the night were delighted the next morning to see soldiers apparently from the Sixth Armored. "We pulled into that area," said John Jarvie, "and the guys said, 'They're bringing heavy tanks in here, just what we need.' And they came running and said, 'Boy, are we happy to see you guys.'"

The third notional task force set up a phantom artillery unit. Dummy artillery pieces were set up six hundred to eight hundred yards in front of the Thirty-Seventh Field Artillery Battalion. Flash canisters were used to simulate firing at night. The canisters consisted of artillery shell casings filled with a half pint of black powder and set off with an electrical igniter. Telephone lines were run between the real artillery and the Ghost Army's phony batteries to synchronize the real firing with the phony flashes. The fake artillery operated for three nights and received twenty to twenty-five rounds of enemy fire, whereas the real artillery received none.

In many ways the deception was a success. "Visual effects were thorough and complete for both enemy air observations and/or enemy agents or patrols," reported Colonel Cyrus Searcy, VIII Corps chief of staff. As for the sonic deception, Searcy noted that an American engineering unit more than a mile away heard enough to convince them that tanks were assembling. The enemy seemed to be getting the message as well. Intelligence officers reported that the Germans shifted from twenty to fifty 88mm antitank guns to meet what they evidently believed to be a major armored threat. After the fall of Brest, General Ramcke told interrogators that he was convinced there really was an armored division facing him. In fact, it was just the illusionists of the Ghost Army.

But the deception did not achieve the goal of bluffing Ramcke into an early surrender. He had about twice as many troops as the Americans thought he did, and they fought on for four more weeks. Furthermore,

Sagging Gun at Sunrise by
Arthur Shilstone, 1944

in the minds of most Ghost Army veterans any success they could claim was overshadowed by the deadly consequences of an American attack mistakenly launched right where the Ghost Army was attracting German attention.

The Commander of the VIII Corps, General Troy Middleton, ordered a general attack on the Germans to take place on August 25 at 1:00 p.m. Bob Tompkins had a front-row seat for the action.

August 25, 1944

    Fireworks start. Artillery raising hell - stood on a hedgerow and watched the whole show. Saw shells landing about 400 yards in front of us, could hear machine guns, rifles, mortars, etc.

— Diary of Sergeant Bob Tompkins

Due to a lack of communication, or perhaps a failure to appreciate the impact of the deception, one company of light tanks moved in on the Germans from precisely the area where the Ghost Army had been simulating a tank battalion. German 88mm antitank weapons drawn by the deception opened fire on the real American tanks. "Those guys never reached the line of departure," recalled Corporal John Jarvie. "They just got decimated."

Jarvie had a close call of his own during the same attack. He was watching from a jeep on a nearby hill when he heard a couple of shells headed his way. "I thought, 'Holy shit, I got to get out of here.' And I tried to get out of the jeep, and my gun belt caught on the wheel. I couldn't get out." The two shells slammed into the ground a few feet from his jeep. Luckily for Jarvie, they turned out to be duds. "Plunk, plunk. Dirt went up in the air and no explosion. That was one of my nine lives."

The incident of the light tanks being devastated weighed heavily on the men in the unit long after they pulled out on August 27. Jarvie was especially haunted by the fact that the GIs manning those tanks undoubtedly thought they would be supported by the heavier tanks of the Sixth Armored Division. "We had no way of knowing they were going to kick off an attack," said Jarvie, "and they had no way of knowing that we weren't going to help them. And it makes you feel lousy." It was a lesson to Lieutenant Colonel Clifford Simenson, the Twenty-Third's operations officer, on the crucial importance of careful coordination and communication. Without them, the results could be catastrophic. The tanks "should not have attacked in that place," he later wrote in an analysis of the operation, "or otherwise the 23rd should have employed deception in another area." They would take what they learned at Brest and put it into practice in future operations.

(opposite) *Normandy, June 1944* by Ellsworth Kelly, 1944

Only half the unit was involved in the deceptions at Brest. The rest set up camp on the grounds of an old château near the Brittany town of Torcé. While their compatriots were setting up tanks in the rain or being peppered with German shells, the men in Torcé enjoyed the opportunity to sample French cuisine and eat in restaurants for the first time since they had arrived in France.

Torcé was the only town in all Europe that was formally "liberated" by the Twenty-third. It was an impressive ceremony. There was a crack American color guard from the Sig Co Sp, a band of French firemen, a pretty white column of schoolchildren with flowers and leading citizens. Col. Reeder delivered a gallant speech, which ended with a rousing VIVE LA FRANCE! Torceans were visibly moved and their rendition of "La Marseillaise" was all the more thrilling from four years of silence.

— Official History of the 23rd Headquarters Special Troops

Somewhere in France by Cleo Hovel, 1944

Reuniting after Operation Brest, the Ghost Army geared up for another deception to aid General George Patton's Third Army, but Patton's forces were pressing ahead so fast that it was called off before it even began. Optimism ran high that they might be headed home soon. "Speculation has it that the war will be over in a month or so," wrote Private Harold Laynor to his wife. "Pray to God there is…some foundation in this." Around September 1 they bivouacked in Mauny near the city of Sens. Low on gas, the 406th Combat Engineers sent out a reconnaissance team to find a fuel depot. But the fuel they discovered was of a different nature. The patrol stumbled across a Wehrmacht warehouse filled with wine and liquor.

The military significance of this was lost on no one. Several "deuce and a half" cargo trucks (each capable of carrying two and a half tons) were duly dispatched, without the inconvenience of explaining to senior officers what was going on. The warehouse was under the watchful eye of a French guard, but he was persuaded by a few cartons of Chesterfield cigarettes to look the other way. The liberated booze was brought back to the unit and distributed to all hands.

> By clever manipulation, the Twenty-third was able to garner 520 cases (6240 bottles) of Cognac. This was enough liquid to drive one jeep 22,000 miles if Cognac would explode. And don't think it wouldn't. So this bivouac area is referred to as "Cognac Hill."
> — Official History of the 23rd Headquarters Special Troops

Robert A. George by Jack Masey, 1944

The trucks brought back more than cognac, according to Lieutenant Dick Syracuse. "They were loaded to the gunnels with Cointreau, calvados, brandy, you name it.... We had a five-hundred-gallon wooden cask of Moselle wine that we used to use instead of water."

The men saw it as their patriotic duty to drink up. "We saved the Germans a lot of work by taking care of it," laughed Sergeant Spike Berry. Private Harold Dahl sent a label from one of the bottles home to his family. "While it was not the best of cognac, it still was a pleasure to have it," he wrote.

Due to their lack of fuel (at least for the engines), the unit remained in their bivouac for four more days, most of which were spent in various states of lubrication. According to Lieutenant Fred Fox, the drinking went all the way to the top. "The colonel lost control completely. For three days he had a drunken mutiny on his hands, but he did not care, either."

Then came gas to fill their tanks and orders to clear their heads. The news was exciting for everyone, especially for the young artists in the 603rd. They were moving out. Their destination: the glittering art and culture capital of the world, just liberated from the Germans.

Paris!

Ghost Army GIs in liberated Paris, 1944

8

A GREAT TOWN

On every block you can see at least
one soldier surrounded by girls, leafing frantically
through French-English dictionaries.

— Lieutenant Fred Fox in a letter home

Hey-- by Cleo Hovel, 1944

On August 25, 1944, the city of Paris was liberated from more than four years of German occupation. Parisians were still celebrating two weeks later when the Twenty-Third Headquarters Special Troops pulled in to the nearby suburb of Saint-Germain-en-Laye, home of the great château that had been the residence of many French kings. The troops lived in an old school that boasted showers and tennis courts, considering themselves to be in the lap of luxury. Better yet, for a few wonderful days they would have a chance to savor the pleasures of a Paris still giddy with euphoria.

Paris was put OFF LIMITS and ON LIMITS so often
that everyone in confusion visited it whenever
possible. It was a great town. Architecturally
it had not changed at all. The girls looked like
delightful dolls especially when they whizzed
past on bicycles with billowing skirts. They were
in considerable contrast to the red-faced Norman
farmer[s'] daughters. The Parisians were very
happy to see us.
— Official History of the 23rd Headquarters Special Troops

Everyone wanted to make the trip into the City of Light. "There were still snipers and things going on in Paris, but we were sneaking in," recalled Lieutenant Dick Syracuse. For Private William Sayles it was "the high point" of his time in Europe. Private Harold Dahl made good use of the

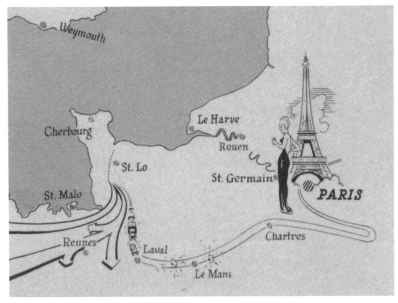

(top) Parisians cheering
Allied troops marching
through the newly liberated
city, August 1944

(bottom) Detail of the
operations map of the
Twenty-Third Headquarters
Special Troops, 1945

(top left and bottom right)
Ghost Army GIs discovering
Paris, 1944

(top right and bottom left)
Creative Cycling sketches by
Victor Dowd, 1944

one day he made it to town. He rode the Métro and walked under the Eiffel Tower, through the Place Vendôme, along the Rue de la Paix, past the Opéra, and along the Seine. Sergeant Bob Tompkins and his buddies parked a truck in front of Notre Dame cathedral and then walked to the Arc de Triomphe, where two Frenchmen offered to give them a tour of the city. "Little sixteen-year-old girl presented me with her own key to the city," he noted in his secret diary. Private Ellsworth Kelly

(left) *Paris, '44* by Cleo Hovel, 1944

(right) *Huguette* by Richard Morton, 1945. Morton painted nineteen-year-old Huguette Guérende while on a three-day leave in Paris in February 1945. He had met her sister, Nicole, during the liberation of Paris in 1944, and had corresponded with Nicole throughout the war.

wandered the streets of Paris alone, numbed by the experience. His friend Bill Griswold somehow finagled an invitation to Picasso's studio, but he didn't offer to bring Kelly along. Kelly was so shy that Griswold thought he would be awkward in the presence of the great artist. Kelly would return to Paris after the war courtesy of the GI Bill. It was there that he developed the minimalist style for which he became famous.

"Paris has an altogether different aura about it," wrote Private Harold Laynor to his wife. "The girls of Paris are different than [in] any other part of France. As a group they are the most beautiful and cute I have ever seen—bar one—you." Lieutenant Fred Fox noted the "fantastic hairdos" and "rainbow blouses" that had a tendency to bewitch Americans. "On every block you can see at least one soldier surrounded by girls, leafing frantically through French-English dictionaries." In the coming months Parisians would grow indifferent and even hostile toward American soldiers, but in these first weeks after liberation, they welcomed the GIs with open arms. "The people are at once more friendly and more deeply grateful to the Yanks than in any other part of France," marveled Laynor. Harold Dahl penned similar sentiments to his mother. "The American soldier is something fabulous to them."

Sergeant Victor Dowd's experiences with the girls of Paris began in Saint-Germain-en-Laye, where he and some other GIs went to a brothel. "It was a great opportunity for me to draw," he recalled with a straight face. "I'm not Toulouse-Lautrec, but here were these women in their underwear. A woman named Doris sat on my table. She had a glass of wine in her hand and a cigarette in the other hand, high heels, and practically no clothes on. And she was trying to entice me to go upstairs. And I wouldn't have had to pay anything if I gave her the drawing. But I wasn't particularly anxious to go upstairs with Doris, and I decided to keep the drawing."

An eccentric British veteran from World War I living in Saint-Germain-en-Laye brought out a motorcycle with a sidecar and offered to bring Dowd into Paris. "I'll never forget driving along the Champs-Élysées and seeing the Arc de Triomphe coming closer and closer." Dowd filled his sketchbook with the girls of Paris. He sketched one girl in a cafe; later they found themselves walking down the street arm in arm. (Dowd's stories frequently involved a girl on his arm. "It sounds like I'm Casanova—maybe it was the sketchbooks!") He heard someone yell, "Hey, Vic," and looked up. It was a kid he used to play stickball with in Brooklyn, now serving in the Air Force. He was hoping Dowd's female companion could provide a girl for him. "That was not in the cards," commented Dowd, and so they soon parted ways, Dowd holding tight to his new friend and letting his old buddy fend for himself.

Victor Dowd's sketches from
a brothel in Saint-Germaine-
en-Laye

A card for the famous Paris brothel Aux Belles Poules (The Beautiful Chicks), picked up by a Ghost Army soldier who visited there

Unlike Dowd, Corporal Arthur Shilstone made very few drawings in Paris because, he said, he was "busy." Doing what, he was asked years later? "We all have our military secrets," he replied, before unbuttoning just a bit. "We got in every night and then came back pretty drunk and then started in the next day and the next night in Paris and so forth."

Lieutenant Bob Conrad and four other officers commandeered a jeep and headed into town the day after they arrived. "This was the day we were going to imbibe the vibes of Paris." Looking for Notre Dame cathedral, they were hailed by an American woman whom they asked for directions. She told them that General Eisenhower was taking part in a great celebration that day at the Arc de Triomphe and suggested they go there instead. "You can see that old church any time." They followed her advice. All were wearing Signal Corps uniforms, and since they were now practiced in the art of deception, they pretended to be Signal Corps photographers in order to get close. They watched as General Eisenhower laid a wreath on the Tomb of the Unknown Soldier. When the band struck up "La Marseillaise," Conrad was "close to tears. It was really very moving. Eventually we over liberated the French, but at that point they loved us."

```
Perfume and fineries were fairly easy to buy and the prices
did not become terrible until later. Cigarettes, D-ration
chocolate and K-ration cheese made welcome gifts. Many
friends were made. While driving down the Champs Élysées
with a jeep-load of fashionable civilians, one had a
tendency to think that the war was over.
```
— Official History of the 23rd Headquarters Special Troops

That thought was at the back of everyone's mind. With Paris liberated and the Germans on the run, surely the war couldn't last much longer. Then, all too soon, reality intruded, and the idyllic interlude in Paris came to an abrupt halt. The war was anything but over. The Ghost Army was ordered to make a mad dash halfway across France, to the very border with Germany, in order to once more lend a hand to General George Patton's Third Army. It was to be one of their most desperate gambles of the war.

Notre Dame by Arthur
Singer, 1945

Dummy tank in position at Bettembourg

9

ONE BAD SPOT IN MY LINE

[I heard] enormous sounds of tracks racing
through the forest, sounded like a whole division
was amassing. Loudspeakers blaring, sergeants' voices
yelling, "Put out that goddamned cigarette now."
It was all fakery—it was all a big act.

— Sergeant Victor Dowd

General George Patton was famous for his gruff tone, salty language, pearl-handled revolvers, and unwavering commitment to the offensive. "In case of doubt, attack!" was one of his favorite dictums. After sweeping out of Brittany in mid-August, Patton's Third Army raced across France, all the way to the Moselle River and the border with Germany, stopping only when fuel ran low and German resistance stiffened.

Patton massed his troops for an attack on the French fortified city of Metz, leaving a dangerous seventy-mile gap to the north. The area was very thinly held by Colonel James Polk's Third Cavalry Group (Mechanized). The Germans were starting to pull together after their disorganized flight through France. "If the Germans realized that there were effectively no troops in the seventy-mile-wide stretch, they could have broken through easily," says military historian Jonathan Gawne. "If they could have gotten some of their mechanized units there, they could have surrounded Patton at Metz to the south. This was a very severe risk." The Twenty-Third was called on to ride to the rescue. Its ambitious mission: plug the hole in the line by once again pretending to be the Sixth Armored Division, which was still working its way east. It would prove to be one of the unit's most risky operations.

They drove 250 miles from Paris to get there. They passed through the great World War I battlefield of Verdun and crossed from France into Luxembourg. In the city of Esch-sur-Alzette, crowds of people lined the streets, cheering this American unit headed toward the front, having no idea what was hidden in their canvas-covered half-tracks and closed-up trucks. On the night of September 15 they pulled in near

Metz by Alvin Shaw, 1944

the Luxembourg town of Bettembourg, just south of Luxembourg City. Sergeant Bob Tompkins was apprehensive about being so close to the front, with very few fighting troops around—not to mention that no one seemed to know exactly where the front line was. Two miles east was the best they could determine. After a few hours of fitful sleep, they leaped into their newest role the next morning.

> September 16, 1944
>   Pulled into the woods at 3 o'clock. Tanks moving all around us. Woke early. Put on patches. Set up tanks. Built fires simulating armored infantry battalion. Truck goes out every hour to village for atmosphere. Drank a quart of beer with a family in Bettembourg.
> — Diary of Sergeant Bob Tompkins

Only twenty-three dummy tanks were set up for Operation Bettembourg. Allied air superiority was reducing German aerial observation, so visual deception was becoming less important. Radio, sonic, and special effects were the key means of carrying out the deception.

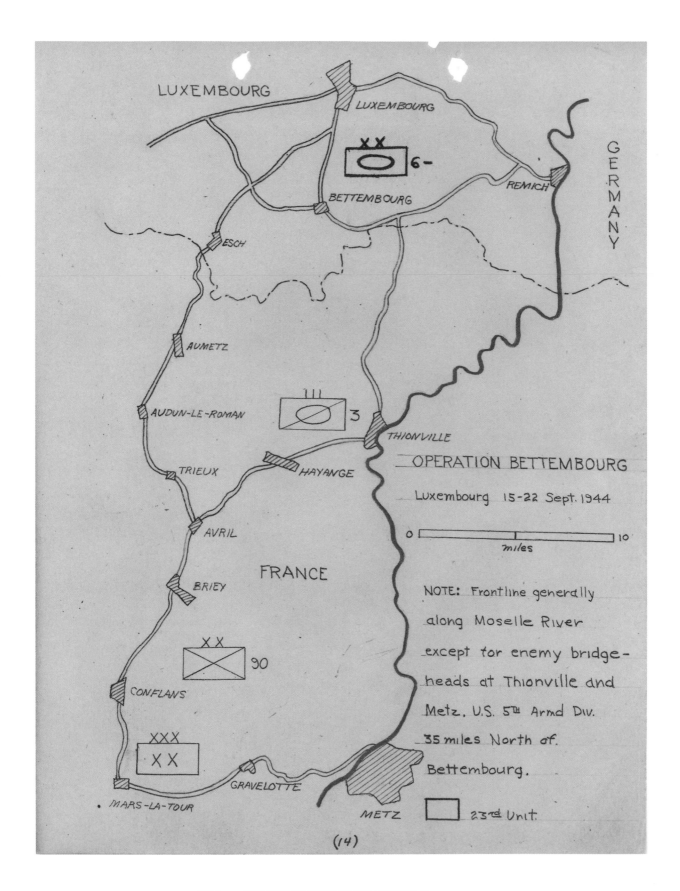

LUXEMBOURG

LUXEMBOURG

XX
6-

BETTEMBOURG

REMICH

GERMANY

ESCH

AUMETZ

AUDUN-LE-ROMAN

III
3

THIONVILLE

TRIEUX

HAYANGE

OPERATION BETTEMBOURG

Luxembourg 15-22 Sept. 1944

0   10
miles

AVRIL

FRANCE

BRIEY

XX
90

NOTE: Frontline generally
along Moselle River
except for enemy bridge-
heads at Thionville and
Metz. U.S. 5ᵗʰ Armd Div.
35 miles North of.
Bettembourg.

CONFLANS

XXX
X X

GRAVELOTTE

MARS-LA-TOUR

METZ

23ʳᵈ Unit.

(14)

With the Germans so close, just across the Moselle River, sonic deception was particularly crucial. Sonic trucks operated for four straight nights.

Listening at night, Sergeant Victor Dowd heard "enormous sounds of tracks racing through the forest, sounded like a whole division was amassing. Loudspeakers blaring, sergeants' voices yelling, 'Put out that goddamned cigarette now.' It was all fakery—it was all a big act."

Lieutenant Dick Syracuse's platoon was manning a security perimeter around the sound trucks as they played their concert of tanks moving in. All of a sudden a colonel from the cavalry unit came "storming up the road," Syracuse recalled. "This guy looked like a monster because he had a flak jacket on, and there were hand grenades hanging, and [he was] carrying a Thompson submachine gun."

"What the hell is going on here, son?"

"What do you mean, Colonel?" replied Syracuse.

"What are those tanks doing there?"

Syracuse tried to explain that there were no tanks actually there. The response was a string of expletives.

"Don't tell me that! I know what I hear! There are tanks out there, and nobody told me there was going to be tanks here!"

Things were eventually straightened out. It developed that the colonel had missed the briefing where the deception was explained, and his aide had not had time to tell him about it yet. His parting words to Syracuse were: "Well, son, you certainly could have fooled me."

Spending long nights doing security for the sonic unit, often stationed between the sonic trucks and the enemy, Syracuse sometimes found himself being fooled. "My eyes were beginning to tell me what my ears were hearing," he recalled. "Psychologically it was the most unnerving thing; I would actually begin to see tanks in the dark."

Radio was also a big part of the deception. Ghost Army operators created three phony networks and interacted with two real ones. Numerous special-effects ploys were staged. Bumper markings and patches were changed. All of the men were given a short history of the Sixth Armored Division and were sent into nearby towns, supposedly on recreation leave, where they could be overheard talking about their division in cafes and bars. Soldiers from the 406th guarded intersections dressed as MPs from the Sixth Armored. "Civilians were

Lieutenant Dick Syracuse

Special Effects by Arthur Shilstone, 1985. Two men would ride in back of the canvas-covered truck to make it appear as if it were full.

(left) *Put the Top Down!* by Walter Arnett, 1945

(right) *France '44* by James Steg, 1944

(opposite) A diagram showing how real and Ghost Army units (called "Blarney" units in this drawing) were connected by telephone wire to the Twentieth Corps headquarters. The Signal Company Special often had to lay down hundreds of miles of wire for every operation. These were used for secure communications, while the radio was used to deceive the enemy.

observed photographing bumpers, taking notes, and asking 'friendly' questions," wrote Lieutenant Colonel Clifford Simenson. The men were under orders not to drink alcohol on these missions, but that particular injunction was more honored in the breach than the observance. "I was never able, while in town, to catch anyone in my command drinking," wrote Captain Oscar Seale in his official report, "but I am sure some drinking was done."

Operation Bettembourg was originally only supposed to last for two days, until the Eighty-Third Infantry Division could arrive to fill the hole. But the Eighty-Third was delayed, so the deception stretched out for day after perilous day. Every passing hour increased the odds that the Germans might see through the deception. German infantry divisions were moving in across the river, presumably to defend against the Sixth Armored Division. The mood grew tense. As Lieutenant Bob Conrad put it, there was nothing between the Ghost Army and the Germans "but our hopes and prayers." Ralph Ingersoll of the Special Plans branch, now a major, visited to warn that the enemy was regrouping and becoming more aggressive. Civilians reported seeing Germans in nearby woods. Shots were heard. Telephone wires laid by the Signal Company were found cut.

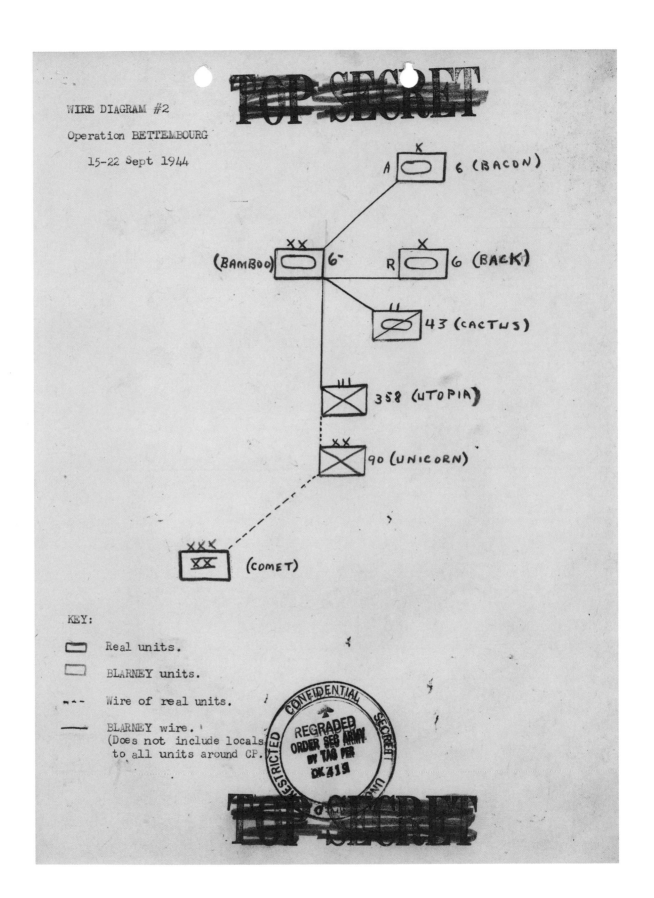

WIRE DIAGRAM #2

Operation BETTEMBOURG

    15-22 Sept 1944

A | K | 6 (BACON)

(BAMBOO) | XX | 6·   R | X | 6 (BACK)

43 (CACTUS)

358 (UTOPIA)

90 (UNICORN)

XXX | XX | (COMET)

KEY:

⬡   Real units.

▭   BLARNEY units.

‐ ‐ ‐   Wire of real units.

———   BLARNEY wire.
(Does not include locals
to all units around CP.

(top) *Near Metz* by George
Vander Sluis, 1944

(bottom) *Poor Little Farmhouse*
by Ned Harris, 1944

120   **THE GHOST ARMY OF WORLD WAR II**

(left) *Home Near Metz* by
Arthur Shilstone, 1944. The
German line is by the last line
of trees.

(right) Bill Blass (left) and Bob
Tompkins in a dugout left by
the Germans

September 21, 1944
    Heinie [German] patrol reported about three or four
miles away. Platoon of 406 went out to look for them.
Civilians seem to be getting too anxious about our set-up.
We should have moved out a couple of days ago, but attack
seems imminent, so I guess we have orders to remain
until it begins.
— Diary of Sergeant Bob Tompkins

Even General Patton was feeling the pressure. He commented on
the situation (without mentioning the Ghost Army) in a letter to his
wife the same day Bob Tompkins was writing in his diary: "There is
one rather bad spot in my line, but I don't think the Huns know it. By
tomorrow night I will have it plugged. Jimmy Polk is holding it now
by the grace of God and a lot of guts." The very next day the Eighty-
Third Division arrived on the scene, and the men of the Ghost Army
gladly relinquished that part of the line.

Operation Bettembourg was the Ghost Army's longest deception of
the war and their most successful one to date. Colonel Simenson considered it a turning point for the unit. "It was our first operation that
was executed fully professionally and correctly." The Ghost Army was
now practiced in the art of deception. The question remained: How long
could they continue their front-line theatrics and remain untouched
by the carnage of war?

Luxembourg, 1944

10

THEY EVEN HAD ART SUPPLIES

Man, we used a lot of fuel. We traveled more across Europe than any other army unit.

— Corporal Al Albrecht

In the back of his German phrase book, Sergeant Stanley Nance kept a list of operations and units impersonated. On the right-hand side is a cheat sheet noting what information was required for each radio deception.

In late September 1944, the Twenty-Third Headquarters Special Troops relocated to Luxembourg City shortly after it was liberated. The streets were lined with cheering crowds and United States flags as they drove in. For the next three months the city served as their base for deception missions up and down the front. Most of the unit was housed in a seminary building that is now part of the University of Luxembourg's Limpertsberg campus. The Germans who previously had occupied the building had absconded with the furniture but left the walls covered with what Lieutenant Fred Fox called "atrocious Nazi murals." The headquarters company (consisting of the Twenty-Third's high-ranking officers and their support staff) and the sonic company bivouacked at a school across town.

For the next few months they lived disjointed lives, shuttling back and forth from dangerous operations near the front to the relative calm of Luxembourg City. They racked up the miles, traveling north as far as Malmedy, Belgium, and south as far as Metz, France. Sometimes they were in all three countries in one day. "Man, we used a lot of fuel," recalled Corporal Al Albrecht. "We traveled more across Europe than any other army unit." Much of the travel was done at night to avoid notice by spies. They drove with covers on their headlights that left only a tiny sliver of light: "cat's eyes," they were called. "We were getting to sleep at two or

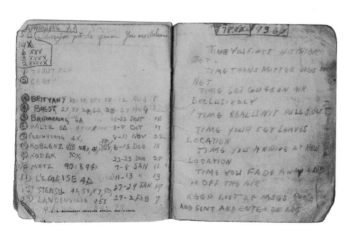

(left) *Luxembourg Bivouac* by Victor Dowd, 1944

(right) *Drying Gear* by Arthur Singer, 1944

Bob Tompkins (at the wheel) and George Martin stuck in Metz mud

three o'clock in the morning," recalled Private First Class Bill Blass, "often in a tent or mud hut flooded with rain."

The autumn rains had come, making a miserable mess of roads and fields. "It was very wet and very cold," said Corporal Arthur Shilstone, "and the trucks were just constantly stuck in the mud, and they'd have to be winched out." Deception operations, having already lost their novelty, now became grueling and exhausting. Sergeant Bob Tompkins summed it up in his diary: "It's muddy as shit, by the way, and very cold."

In any given deception, a soldier rarely had any idea what was going on beyond his specific job. The radio men didn't know what the *camoufleurs* were doing, and all that either of those units knew about the sonic company's efforts was what they heard at night. Lieutenant Gil Seltzer, a platoon leader in the 603rd, recalled being told that if any men approached one of the sonic trucks without permission, they risked being shot. Lieutenant Bernie Mason just focused on whatever task he was given. "We never did have the big picture.... All we did was what we were told to do." Enlisted men like Bob Tompkins were even more in the dark. "One part of our unit might be in a

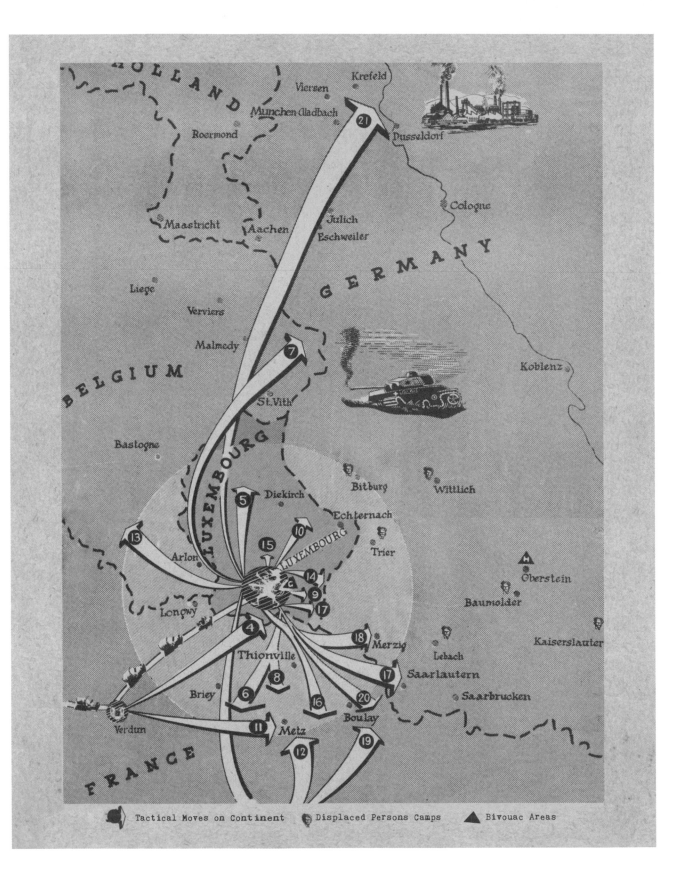

Tactical Moves on Continent   Displaced Persons Camps   Bivouac Areas

field three hundred yards this way and somebody else over here. And we never knew what we were doing or why we were doing it."

Danger was ever present. They frequently drew artillery fire while carrying out their deceptions. "We made sure that we had our foxholes deep, and we kept ourselves as safe as we could," said Mason. "One slip might have meant our necks," Corporal Sebastian Messina recalled after the war. Corporal Albrecht never forgot how frightening it was. "Yes, we were scared. We didn't know whether we would come back the next day or not. It was possible that [each] mission was going to be our last mission. While we weren't firing guns or defending ourselves or shooting somebody, we were still vulnerable to attack by the German army."

Back in Luxembourg, between missions, everything seemed different. Private Ned Harris thought life was pretty good. "The town was not destroyed and even had art supplies stores!" They wandered down into the scenic Grund, the lower part of the city that the men referred to as "the Gulch." The artists made frequent trips there to sketch and paint its quaint and beautiful environs.

Harris had acquired a German grenade case, which he used to carry around his painting supplies. "And then my finished drawings went in there. So it was a receptacle for death, and I was bringing these lively drawings to fill it up."

(left) Ned Harris with the grenade case he used to carry his art supplies and drawings

(right) Bob Tompkins drawing in the Grund, Luxembourg City, 1944

Lux '44 by William Sayles,
1944

(opposite) *Luxembourg City*
by George Vander Sluis,
1944

Luxembourg by Bob
Tompkins, 1944

(opposite) *City of
Luxembourg* by Belisario
Contreras, 1944

(left) *Aline in Luxembourg* by Victor Dowd, 1944

(right) *Luxembourg* by Bruce Zillmer, 1944

They filled up their sketchbooks, visited with Luxembourg families, gathered souvenirs, and marked time until they had to head into the field once again. Luxembourgers viewed them as liberators and gave them a warm welcome. A woman named Anny Dondelinger wrote a letter to the father of Sergeant Stanley Wright in which she explained why she had invited Wright and a friend to visit her house. "I wanted to give them the thing they yearned for most—a warm friendship and the 'home' they have missed for so long." Many soldiers acquired girl-friends, and at least one, Private Thomas Cuffari, married a young woman from Luxembourg and brought her back to the United States.

Even while awaiting their next assignment, their time was not always their own. They had frequent inspections, physical training hikes, and lectures to attend. Lieutenant Bernie Mason was one of many who could never forget the day Colonel Reeder gathered them all in Luxembourg City's Schobermesse Square—a very public space—to give them a speech on secrecy! "He gave us a lecture on how secretive we had to be…where everybody could hear what he was saying. Obviously, it was almost comical, and it didn't make too much sense." Private Walter Arnett, no fan of Reeder, captured the scene in a devastating cartoon. Arnett was not the only one getting fed up with military life. "Would like to shit on every damn officer in this damned company," Bob Tompkins furiously scribbled in his diary.

(left) *Col. Reeder Addressing the Troops* by Walter Arnett, 1944

(right) Two cartoons by Walter Arnett

While at Fort Meade, Walter Arnett and Richard Morton became the camp cartoonists. Walter recalls: "The fellows loved our cartoons, and the officers encouraged us on since it did give the boys something to think about and get their minds off bitching about the Army.... One big skinny boy [Ziebe] from Jacksonville, Fla, offered much material [for the cartoonists].... He didn't like them much and became quite angry a few times.... The bulletin board...became the gathering place for the fellows to see who 'made' the board that week...." Many of the subjects of their lampoons were officers, who were less than thrilled. In this memo Colonel Otis Fitz and Major William D. Hooper tried to end the cartooning careers of Arnett and Morton. Fortunately for them, General Eisenhower issued an order against the suppression of cartoons.

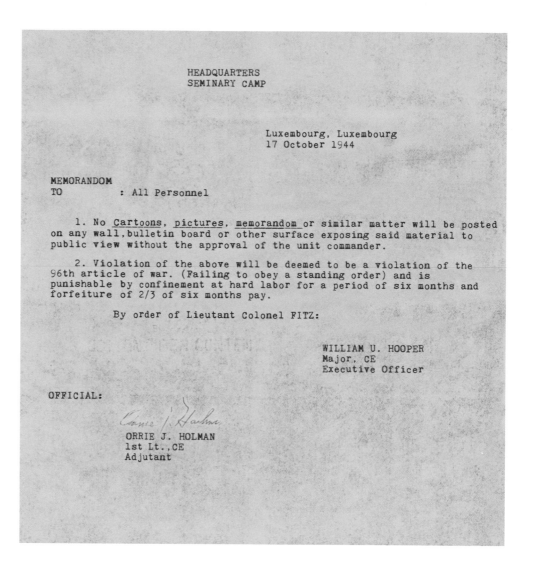

HEADQUARTERS
SEMINARY CAMP

Luxembourg, Luxembourg
17 October 1944

MEMORANDOM
TO   : All Personnel

1. No Cartoons, pictures, memorandom or similar matter will be posted on any wall, bulletin board or other surface exposing said material to public view without the approval of the unit commander.

2. Violation of the above will be deemed to be a violation of the 96th article of war. (Failing to obey a standing order) and is punishable by confinement at hard labor for a period of six months and forfeiture of 2/3 of six months pay.

By order of Lieutant Colonel FITZ:

WILLIAM U. HOOPER
Major, CE
Executive Officer

OFFICIAL:

ORRIE J. HOLMAN
1st Lt., CE
Adjutant

A popular way to pass the time was watching movies. Someone had liberated a 16mm projector, and Lieutenant Fred Fox recruited Sergeant Spike Berry to start what became known as the Blarney Theatre (Blarney being the somewhat revealing code name of the Twenty-Third). Different army corps maintained their own film depots, and Berry borrowed movies from them to show to the Twenty-Third. He found it tough sledding, since no one had ever heard of the unit and he couldn't reveal very much about it. On top of that, because it was relatively small, the unit was always at the bottom of the priority list.

One day, at a film depot, he noticed a bunch of projectors up on a shelf. When he asked about them he was told they were all "dead in the water" because their exciter lamps had burned out. The exciter lamp was a tiny component that played the soundtrack. It seemed silly to Berry that something so small should be sidelining those projectors. He wrote to General Electric, getting their address off a nameplate on a projector, and asked if they could spare some exciter lamps. About a month later he received a box full of them. He suddenly became a popular figure at the film depots and could get any film he wanted. Berry recalled that they always had to return them by 11:00 a.m. the following day to stay in the good graces of the film depot. "That might mean getting up at three or four in the morning and driving, but we got those films back on time."

Sergeant Spike Berry

The irrepressible Sgt Berry helped save the nights with his BLARNEY Theatre. This wasn't the first or last location in which he set up his 16mm "gun," as he called it. He estimates that he shot [projected] 2,741,523 feet of film ...during his tour of the ETO.... Berry maintained his Blarney Theatre in eight different CPs across Europe and toward the end of the war he also had a "mobile unit" which played anywhere.
— Official History of the 23rd Headquarters Special Troops

Even in Luxembourg City, however, the war was never too far away. On October 21, 1944, Sergeant Bob Tompkins saw his first V-1 pilotless buzz bomb, or "robomb," as the soldiers called them, fly overhead. "The first time we saw [one], we didn't know what the hell it was. And it was on its way to England, to London." He saw another one a few days later. He heard the motor cut off and seconds later the explosion, which he estimated was ten miles away. Soon the sight and sound of them were commonplace. And there were other grim reminders of war as well.

November 15, 1944
    Luxembourg becoming a living hell at night. Last week 5 GIs were found dead in the gulch. Shooting every night. Boys arriving from Front for rest. Get drunk and spray street with machine guns. Five civilians killed the other night, still many collaborators working under the cover of darkness.
— Diary of Sergeant Bob Tompkins

After a mission in early November, weeks went by without another operation. Those old enough to vote filled out absentee ballots in the presidential election, where Republican Thomas E. Dewey was trying to prevent President Franklin D. Roosevelt from capturing a fourth term. Bob Tompkins was hoping for and expecting a change at the top. "It would be great to know that Dewey had won," he wrote on election day. "However, have my doubts. Probably won't know until at least the end of the week." Tompkins, of course, was to be disappointed.

Onstage at the seminary: Vaudeville skits in the "Blarney Breakdown" and a performance by Marlene Dietrich

In late October the men put on a talent show at the seminary. Artists from the 603rd decorated the stage, and the "Blarney Breakdown" operated for three straight nights. Another welcome diversion came on November 20, 1944, when Marlene Dietrich came to the seminary and performed in the chapel where the Blarney Breakdown had taken place. The German-born Hollywood actress and singer, who became a United States citizen in 1939, was strongly anti-Nazi. She tirelessly entertained American troops during World War II, often giving concerts very close to the front lines. This was obviously very risky, since as a prominent German native, she would have been dealt with harshly had she fallen into the hands of the Nazis. When asked why she was willing to risk her life this way, she said simply, *"Aus anstand"* (out of decency).

Dietrich sang the soldiers' favorite, "Lili Marlene," and even played the saw. She wore a full-length dress, but, according to Private Richard Morton, "You could still see enough to tell she had a good pair of legs." The room was packed, not only with soldiers from the Ghost Army but also with American officers from other units in Luxembourg. One of those attending was a rear-echelon captain making a tour of the front. Like many of the men in the unit, he too was an artist. Before the war he had worked with Major Ralph Ingersoll, which is probably how he wrangled an invitation to the concert. His name was Theodore Geisel, and he would one day become world famous under the pen name he was already using: Dr. Seuss.

Sak as Sophie Tucker by George Vander Sluis, 1944

Several Ghost Army soldiers cherish memories of seeing Dietrich close up. Bob Tompkins nearly knocked her down rushing through the hallway to get to the concert. Bernie Mason recalled introducing her to the crowd. Private William Sayles chuckled at the thought of her entourage. "She was surrounded by all these officer guys who were escorting her wherever she had to go. And she was the queen of the day, let me tell you. She was the queen."

A few days later, many of the deceivers sat down for a Thanksgiving dinner in the same room. "Real honest to goodness turkey!" Private Harold Dahl enthused in a letter home. But it wasn't enough to drive away the weary homesickness. "I'd rather have cold lamb there than turkey here, believe you me," he wrote his mother. Around the same time, one soldier in the camouflage unit had too much to drink and accidentally shot and wounded one of his compatriots. Everyone was getting edgy, wondering when the wretched war might come to an end. Several weeks earlier, Dahl had summed up the mood in a letter home:

October 15, 1944

What keeps those Germans going is beyond us — they've lost almost everything in the way of sources of supply, army after army, and still they prolong what must inevitably end in their complete surrender. All they are doing in causing more men to die, more women & children, German this time, to go homeless for a dead cause. Surely there must be some in Germany who see clearly what they are up against or must we beat it into every skull individually? Let's hope it will soon clear up.

You on K.P.!

Corporal Jack Masey decided to use the time between
missions to caricature the men of his company. "I'm going
to capture every one of these crazies," he told himself.
He put them all together in a book called *You on K.P.!*
(KP, or Kitchen Patrol, was a dreaded duty that often was
given out as a punishment; it involved such tasks as peeling
potatoes or washing dishes.) He collected money from his
buddies and found a printer in Luxembourg City who ran
off a copy for every soldier in Company B of the 603rd.
They autographed one another's books and saved them as
souvenirs. These are from Private William Sayles's copy.

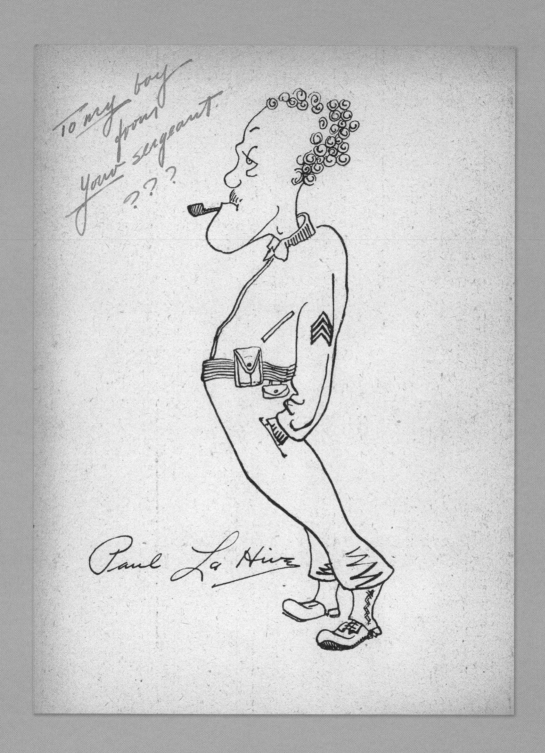

Mordecai R. Craig

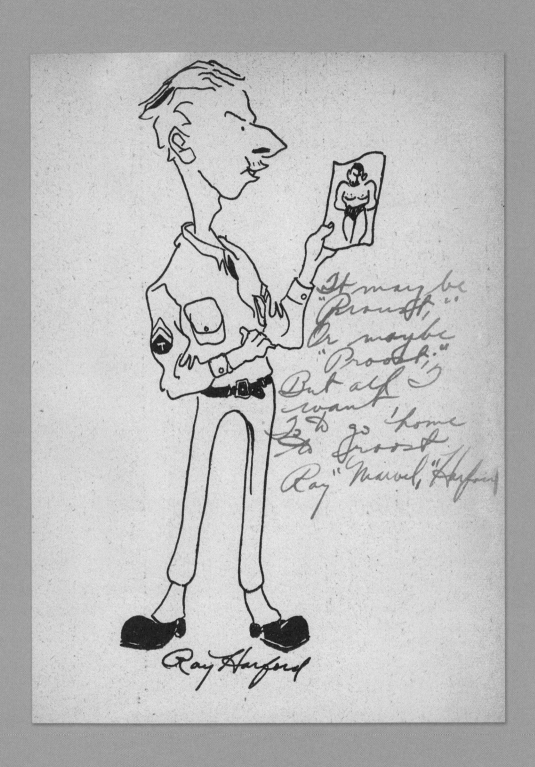

George "Hinkle" Martin

Noo, what more can I say. It really was that long. 3 years + in the 603rd. I'll always remember the days. The same old story etc. Good Luck to you, Bill, always "Hinkle"

Ghost Army soldiers in the snow in Luxembourg, 1944

11

ALL THEIR HEAVY HITTERS

Victory looks like it's in sight. The Allies are pushing like crazy.
Then, whammo! Out of nowhere: "Pack up. We're going.
The Germans are coming." It was a very depressing moment.

— Corporal Jack Masey

n December 1944 the Ghost Army headed out on what seemed like
just another mission, their sixth since arriving in Luxembourg. There
had been heavy fighting up north, as the Allies captured the German
city of Aachen and then launched a bloody attack through the Hürtgen
Forest. But farther south, a ninety-mile section of the front along the
rugged Ardennes Forest was thinly held by just four American divisions.

The Twenty-Third was brought in to help bolster the line. Their mission was to impersonate the Seventy-Fifth Infantry Division moving
into the area northeast of Luxembourg City. The hope was to prevent
Germans from transferring troops out of that area and perhaps force
them to take troops away from the fight in Hürtgen Forest to deal with
the perceived threat of the Seventy-Fifth.

Colonel Billy Harris, chief of the Twelfth Army Group's Special
Plans branch, was against the deception. He thought the situation had
changed too much for plans worked out weeks earlier to be effective.
But Colonel Harry L. Reeder was anxious to keep his men busy, since
they had not carried out a deception in nearly a month. And VIII Corps
Commander General Troy Middleton, overseeing that section of the
front, was happy to have some reinforcements, even if it was a "rubber duck" division, as he called it. So Operation Koblenz was com-
menced—"without a real hope on anybody's part for success," according
to Harris.

The Ghost Army played all its usual tricks. Phony Seventy-Fifth
Infantry Division convoys moved along the roads to villages east and
northeast of Luxembourg City, while the radio and sonic units made
it seem as if triple that number of vehicles were moving in. Phony

command posts were set up, and phony MPs directed traffic. Colonel Reeder put on general's stars and visited each of the fake headquarters, impersonating Seventy-Fifth Division commander General Fay Prickett. Private Harold Dahl found it amusing that because the Seventy-Fifth was supposed to be new to the area, "We had to listen politely while being told all about Luxembourg City and give the impression of ignorance when actually we had left there the day before."

One goal of the deception was to convince the Germans that the Seventy-Fifth was about to attack across the Sauer River. Lieutenant Colonel Otis Fitz, Commander of the 603rd, and Captain George Rebh, commander of the 406th, led a two-jeep patrol to a forward position near the town of Girsterklaus, as if they were making a reconnaissance of where the crossing might take place. They parked their jeeps behind a building and started making their way down to some trees by the river. "Shortly after we entered the tree line, bullets started flying over our head. You could hear them hitting the leaves in the trees," recalled Rebh. A firefight broke out, most likely with a German patrol that had crossed to the Allied side of the river to nab some prisoners. Rebh knew it would be disastrous for them to be taken, so he ordered a hasty withdrawal.

The discovery of an aggressive German patrol was, perhaps, an indication that this sector wasn't nearly as quiet as it seemed. The Ghost Army was about to get caught up in one of the biggest battles that American troops fought during World War II: the Battle of the Bulge. "The Germans were coming in, getting ready for the Bulge," recalled Corporal John Jarvie. "They were putting all their heavy hitters in there, and we didn't know it."

Corporal John Jarvie

While the 23rd thought they were waving a red flag at a suckling calf, a Nazi bull was preparing to charge. Instead of Luxembourg being the dullest sector with school troops and resting veterans, it soon hit the headlines of the world when two raging Panzer Armies drove into the "Bulge."
— Official History of the 23rd Headquarters Special Troops

German intelligence noted the possible presence of the Seventy-Fifth Infantry Division on their maps for a few days and then decided that it wasn't really there. But it made little difference. Hitler had been planning the massive surprise attack for months, as a last-ditch attempt to win the war. In the early morning hours of December 16, three German armies launched a massive counterattack in the Ardennes. Dazed American units along the front barely knew what hit them, and soon the retreat was on.

Units from the Twenty-Third prepare to retreat during the Battle of the Bulge

The attack came as the men of the Twenty-Third were wrapping up the first stage of Operation Koblenz and were preparing to undertake the second stage. Their deception was directly in the path of the German onslaught. On Sunday, December 17, Corporal Jarvie and Company C of the 603rd were in Hoscheid, Luxembourg, about five miles behind the front. They were preparing for the next day's scheduled arrival of a larger contingent of Ghost Army soldiers who would commence the second part of the deception. Jarvie had spent the night in the parish house and, with some other soldiers, attended Mass in the morning. Shortly afterward, the men were alerted that German infantry had broken through and was headed their way. They quickly packed up and pulled back to Luxembourg City, all too aware that capture would expose their deception operation.

Other Ghost Army units also beat a hasty retreat. "We ran like hell," said Private Irving Stempel. "At least, Company D did." Fortunately, most of the men carrying out the first part of Operation Koblenz finished their work before the Germans attacked. "Somebody in their wisdom decided to pull us out," recalled Ed Biow, adding that if they had stayed there, they would have been wiped out. "There'd be no Twenty-Third." Soldiers in nearby American units overwhelmed by the German attack were angry that the Seventy-Fifth Infantry Division, which they thought was right next to them in line, was suddenly nowhere to be found.

In an evacuation hospital a few days after the German counteroffensive began, a soldier from the 4th Infantry was heard to remark: "I'd like to get my hands on those elusive bastards of the Seventy-fifth."
— Official History of the 23rd Headquarters Special Troops

Sergeant Spike Berry found out about the attack while making one of his routine runs to return a movie screened for some of the men in Luxembourg the night before. He drove into the town where the VIII Corps movie library was located. "Film library was closed. Gone, nobody there. I thought, 'Hell, what's going on here?'" Berry went to a square in the middle of the town and saw a military policeman. "I said, 'What's going on here?' He said, 'What the hell are you doing here?' I said, 'I'm returning a movie film.' He said, 'You're returning *what?*' I said, 'I'm returning a movie film.'" The vexed MP advised him to ready the gun normally stowed in the leather holster on the side of the jeep.

"'And then you and your driver get the hell out of town.'" The town was
Bastogne, Belgium, surrounded shortly afterward by the Germans and
soon to earn a place in history for the stand made there by the 101st
Airborne Division.

At the seminary in Luxembourg City, less than twenty miles from the
attacking Germans, word of the offensive arrived on the afternoon of
Sunday, December 17. Sergeant Bob Tompkins was already in a state
of high anxiety. His wife was expecting a baby back in the States. Her
due date was near, and still he had received no word. "Only a matter of
days," he had written in his diary on December 1. "Terribly fidgety," he
scrawled a few days later. Now there was a frightening new worry:

```
December 17, 1944
   Suddenly alerted about 4 o'clock. Germans reported
counter attacking heavily. Reports say Three German
divisions on this side of the river. Supposedly only 8 Km
out of Luxembourg ... loading all special equipment in case
we must pull out. Worried and really low tonight. No word
yet. Nothing seems right. Shit!
```
— Diary of Sergeant Bob Tompkins

Corporal Jack Masey was one of many who found themselves in a
state of disbelief. "Victory looks like it's in sight. The Allies are pushing

like crazy. Then, whammo! Out of nowhere: 'Pack up. We're going. The Germans are coming.' It was a very depressing moment. What's happened? Where did these Germans get this sudden eleventh-hour energy?"

Ghost Army gunners manned machine guns atop the seminary and blazed away at attacking Luftwaffe planes. For most, it was the only time during the war they actually had a chance to fire at the enemy. Trucks were loaded with gear in anticipation of the unit's withdrawal. Lieutenant Bernie Mason, trained in demolition, was given orders to set charges on all the vehicles carrying dummies and other secret equipment to prevent them from being discovered if the enemy overran the city before they could retreat.

The sense of panic was real. But the United States Army held the Twenty-Third in Luxembourg City for a few days in case it would be needed. Finally, word came down on December 21. Most of the Ghost Army would withdraw and head west the next day, away from the front. The radio men, however, along with some of the combat engineers from the 406th, were to go in a different direction. General George Patton's Third Army was on its way to relieve the 101st Airborne Division in Bastogne, and the radio deceivers were going to lend a hand.

Supreme Allied Commander Dwight D. Eisenhower had ordered Patton to execute a complicated pivot and advance two divisions north to break through to Bastogne. With his genius for propelling himself into the center of the action, Major Ralph Ingersoll wrangled an invitation to a meeting in Verdun, at which Twelfth Army Group Commander Omar Bradley, General Patton, and other high-ranking officers were planning the move. Ingersoll recalled that the meeting was "intense." Just after he arrived, a "telephone call came through from Bastogne itself. Bradley had the besieged commander there on the line to ask him if he felt he could not hold out until we could reach through to him."

By a bizarre coincidence, this communication with General Anthony McAuliffe, acting commander of the 101st, and ranking officer in Bastogne, seems to have been patched through by a Ghost Army signalman stuck behind enemy lines. Private First Class William Anderson was in a bombed-out building in Luxembourg, tapping into a "mass of telephone wires" that ran through the building. He and another signalman were so busy monitoring communications and relaying messages that they got left behind when the Twenty-Third retreated. One day, according to Anderson, "the phone rang, and a man asked if we could get through to General Bradley." He told Anderson he was the commanding general in Bastogne, and his troops were surrounded, low on ammunition, and almost out of food. Anderson got Bradley on the line, but had to relay the message because the connection was so weak. Anderson recalled that the general asked Bradley if he should

Map created in 1945 depicting Operation Kodak. It was known as Kodak because it was a "double exposure" operation, showing units to be in two places at once to confuse the Germans.

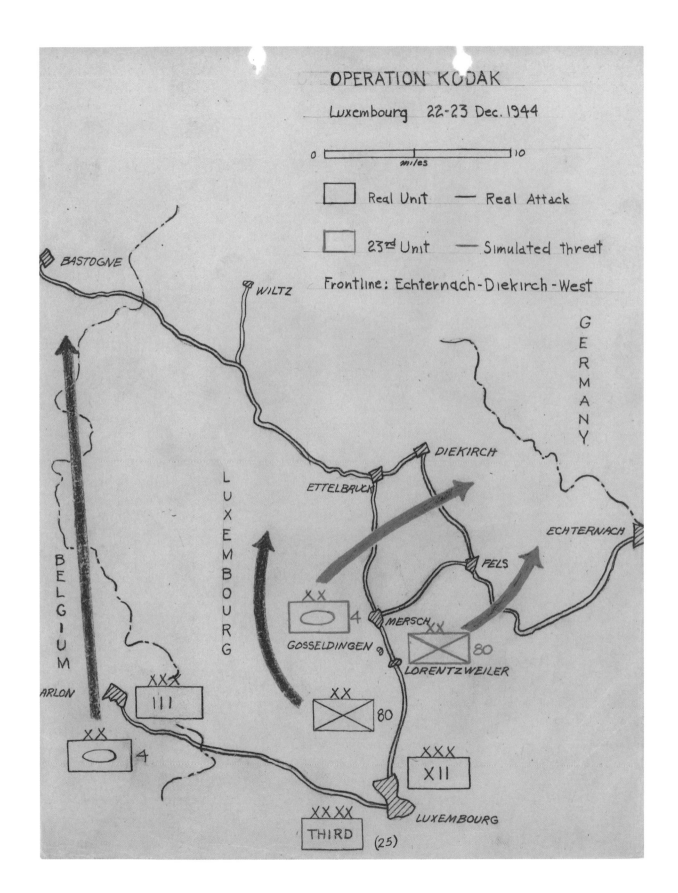

OPERATION KODAK

Luxembourg 22-23 Dec. 1944

```
0 |————————————————| 10
          miles
```

☐ Real Unit —— Real Attack

☐ 23ʳᵈ Unit —— Simulated threat

Frontline: Echternach-Diekirch-West

BASTOGNE

WILTZ

GERMANY

BELGIUM

LUXEMBOURG

DIEKIRCH

ETTELBRUCK

ECHTERNACH

FELS

ARLON

III

MERSCH

GOSSELDINGEN

LORENTZWEILER

4

XX 4

XX 80

XX 80

XXX XII

XXXX THIRD (25)

LUXEMBOURG

surrender or fight it out. General Bradley told Anderson to pass along the message that whatever the general decided, Bradley would understand and not hold it against him. General McAuliffe decided he would hold on, and Bradley wished him luck. Anderson was able to rejoin the Twenty-Third a few days later.

Back at the meeting in Verdun, Ingersoll recalled Patton "striding up and down the room, not the cocky man I remembered, but one with lines of grim concern etched on his face." Bradley was concerned that Patton's movement would be difficult to disguise, and suddenly he turned to Ingersoll. He wanted to know if there was anything the Ghost Army could do to fool the Germans about where Patton would strike. Ingersoll, aware that everyone in the room was looking at him, replied, "Yes, we can do…" and then paused because he didn't know exactly what they could do.

"…something," he added lamely.

"Then do it, " Bradley replied.

Ingersoll and other officers concocted an idea for a hasty radio-only deception that would last just twenty-four hours. While two real divisions, the Fourth and the Eightieth, set out for Bastogne, the Ghost Army would imitate the same divisions going into reserve. The idea was that the German radio operators listening in wouldn't know which were the real divisions and which were the fakes. Twenty-nine Ghost Army radio sets went on the air December 22. Since they were giving the Germans a confusing "double exposure," the mission was called

A Ghost Army radio operator

Operation Kodak. Military historians are unsure about its effectiveness, but Ingersoll never had any doubts. "This bit of trickery I do know *did* work—exactly as conceived," wrote Ingersoll years later. "When the first Third Army Troops hit the flanks of the Bastogne besiegers, the German command was completely confused about where the others might be about to attack." Patton's Third Army broke through the German ring around Bastogne and linked up with the 101st Airborne on December 26.

At the same time, the rest of the Twenty-Third Headquarters Special Troops headed away from the fighting. Private Ed Biow couldn't believe how hard it was snowing. Driving out of Luxembourg, several soldiers spotted panicky Luxembourgers replacing American flags on their houses with swastikas or white flags, in anticipation of the Germans reoccupying the area. "It said something about Europe," recalled Jack Masey. "They were victim to these hordes coming in all directions, and they had to be prepared to survive." Masey said it taught him something about survival. "I probably would have done the same thing, had I been a Luxembourg family."

Private Arnold Marcus in Verdun. Behind him is the Douaumont Ossuary, holding the remains of soldiers who died during the World War I battle.

Christmas 1944. These are soldiers from Company A of the 603rd. Front row center (on bench) is Art Kane, and directly behind him is Ed Biow.

They spent Christmas in the French town of Doncourt-lès-Longuyon. "Still no word from Babe," Bob Tompkins wrote in his diary, waiting for news of the delivery. Then they continued on to Verdun, which Lieutenant Bob Conrad thought "still smelled of World War I." Verdun was the site of the biggest battle in that war, a gruesome set piece in which more than half a million soldiers died. Lieutenant Fred Fox thought it "a depressing city filled with a million ghosts of other unhappy soldiers. That makes it much too crowded." It was in the cold, wet World War I fortifications that they grimly camped out to await their next move.

Some of the men cut Christmas trees. They had to improvise decorations. "One way was to inflate condoms and hang them on there like balloons," recalled Ed Biow. "And the other method was to take tin cans and cut stars out of the tin cans." To bring some joy to their cheerless Christmas, they threw a party for some refugee children.

(top left) GI Double Dutch

(top right) *Belle of the Ball* by
Cleo Hovel, 1944

(bottom) *He Never Smiled*
and *The Sisters, Polish* by
Victor Dowd, 1944

Christmas card made by a
soldier in the 603rd, 1944

December 24, 1944
     Dear Mom & Lou,
Well, we've made a bit of Christmas to start the tears in
our eyes. We managed to fix a tree decorated with garlands
of Christmas paper, imitation candy canes, cards, and
ornaments made out of the bits of metallic paper that is
used to confuse things in air attacks....
     Then we collected a huge amount of candy, gum, rations
& cigarettes, made up several dozen boxes for kids and a
lot for families. We then arranged to have a lot of kids
of Nazi-deported families from eastern Europe come in after
supper and each get a box of exciting things to carry home.
Then we went out with the family boxes and took one to each
of the kids' homes.... Several of those here tonight had
both their parents killed off before that bunch of supermen
shipped the kids over here.
     You will know that I'll be thinking of you on Christmas
and wishing that next year will find me at home.
     Love –
     Harold [Dahl]

Sergeant Victor Dowd was struck by the sad eyes of two Polish
sisters, ages seven and three, and a little boy that no person or present
could cheer up. "I can remember it so vividly. He had had this box,
and it was open. But he was so forlorn looking, and nobody could get
this little boy to smile. God knows what he'd been through."

> When New Year's Eve did come it wasn't particularly gay.
> It is hard to celebrate in dreary, cold, unlighted
> barracks, especially when neither liquor, victory, home,
> nor girls are available.
>
> — Official History of the 23rd Headquarters Special Troops

One Ghost Army soldier *was* in a mood to celebrate. On December 29, Bob Tompkins opened up *Stars and Stripes*, the newspaper published by the army for GIs, and saw the piece of news he had been waiting for. "JUST READ IN STARS AND STRIPES. IT'S A BOY. DECEMBER 18. WOW!!!" he wrote in his diary. But for the rest, it was a holiday largely bereft of good cheer, replaced instead by anxiety.

In many ways 1944 had seemed a heady year. They had crossed the ocean to England, crossed the channel to France, and crossed France to the German border. They had proved they could put on a show that would fool the enemy and stay alive in the process. Then, just when victory seemed within easy reach, they had been forced to retreat to Verdun. Now, amid the cold and snow and a million ghosts, they wondered just what fate awaited them in 1945.

Ned Harris ink sketch and
Arthur Singer watercolor of
the same scene outside their
gloomy Verdun barracks,
part of Fort de Vaux. "It
brought up the whole issue
that war is about life and
death," recalled Harris.
"And we were right in the
middle of it."

Mail Call

During World War II, tons of mail were sent back and forth
across the ocean between soldiers and their loved ones
in the States. Some of the artists in the Ghost Army
illustrated their notes back home. Others chose instead
to sketch their buddies absorbed in reading and writing.
And quite a few letters were sent from Europeans
to the American families of GIs they had befriended.

One popular way to send mail was via V-Mail (*V* for *Victory*).
The original V-Mail was reduced onto microfilm, then
printed back in the United States and mailed to the
recipient, saving shipping space on transatlantic voyages.

Sunday Letter by Cleo
Hovel, 1945

Darling sweet baby there's nothing new — I didn't get a letter today from you & I'm really looking forward to tomorrow's mail call — I'm waiting for the week end as never before — I miss you so much dearest — I love you my precious & always always think of you every minute of the day — Thank God for you my own sweet wonderful wife — God Bless you — I worship you and I need you so — I pray that you will always love me — Your husband

**Letter from Sergeant
Joseph Mack**

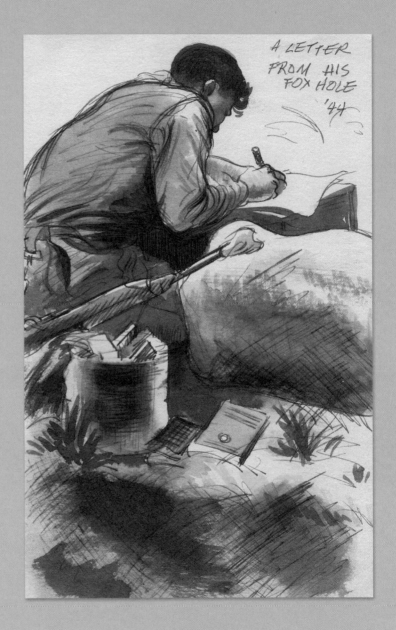

(left) *Chris* by Tony
Young, 1944

(right) *A Letter from His Fox
Hole* by Victor Dowd, 1944

(left) *The Letter* by Walter
Arnett, 1945

(right) *Soldier Reading* by
Paul Seckel

(left) *Be My Valentine* by
Bernie Mason

(right, top) *France Has Some
Pretty Sites* by William Sayles

(right, bottom) *Post-War Plan*
by Joseph Mack

Luxembourg, May 20th 1945.

Dear Mr. Wright!

I suppose I am not a stranger for you as you are none for me.

Your son Stanley told me so often about you and gave me stamps he asked for me and you were so kind to send him for me. My best thanks for your kindness and I will send you soon some new Luxelg. stamps for your collection too. I enclose some Belgian stamps and hope you will enjoy them.

I met your son Stan. in Luxemburg when they came as our "Liberators"; he was in a barake

This letter was written by a young woman named Anny, whose family had befriended Stanley Wright and his group while they were stationed in Luxembourg during the late stages of the war.

near our house and I invited him
to come home with his friend.
I wanted to give them the thing they
yearn for most -- a warm friendship
and "the "home" they have missed
for so long. We spent very pleasant
moments together speaking of you
all, your life and pleasures, playing
music and we became great friends.

For the moment Stan. is living
in Germany with his Comp. but near
the Luxemburg frontiere and they
are allowed to come to Luxembourg
for a Sunday or for 5 hours.
So Stanley came to visit us and
we were happy to celebrate the
V-Day with him and friends of
him with a faithful heart and
we never will forget our Liberators.

The letter is to Wright's father.
It was written shortly after V-E
Day, on May 20, 1945.

"1"

We were thinking at you all
and talking about you, because
all the "American Boys" wished
to be at home at this very moment
and celebrate their victory with
you. We did our best to let them
feel "home" — Stan asked me to
write to you and send you the
pictures we took.

I'll do this with pleasure and
give you good news of your Son.
He is in the best of health and
in good humour — just a little
"homesick" — (now more than
before) as they expect to come
home soon.

We wish for you it will be
soon --- though we will miss
Stan and his friends -- really.

With kindest regards to
You and M⁰ Wright, I am
Sincerely Yours
Kurz

Exp.: Anny DONDELINGER
216 avenue de la FAIENGERIE
LUXEMBOURG.

Wright is third from the left in
this photo taken on V-E Day.

A Ghost Army convoy stops for a break.

12

THE COLDEST WINTER IN FORTY YEARS

There were **days** it seemed to me that we didn't get any sleep.
I would just **have** loved to have gotten up in one of those tanks,
those soft tanks, and gone to sleep.

— Corporal Arthur Shilstone

One thing stuck in Private Ed Biow's memory about the winter of 1944–45. He went forty-three days without taking a bath or shower. The number remained lodged in his brain: forty-three. He was constantly on the move, and "it was so damn cold you didn't care." Forty-three days during which the best he could do was wash his face and hands every once in a while.

By January 1945 the German attack had been blunted and the Allies were back on the offensive. The Ghost Army was called on to conduct a series of deceptions to mask where each new blow would fall. A flurry of missions with names such as Lochinvar, L'Eglise, and Steinsel kept the men of the Twenty-Third in near-constant action.

Once again they were ranging up and down the front for their deception missions. They portrayed the Ninetieth Division, the Fourth Division, and the Ninety-Fifth Division in quick succession. One operation blurred into the next. "There were days it seemed to me that we didn't get any sleep," remembered Corporal Arthur Shilstone. He longed for a comfortable place to get some rest. "I would just have loved to have gotten up in one of those tanks, those soft tanks, and gone to sleep." He chuckled as he went on. "Of course, that would be a court-martial offense."

It was all happening in the harshest of conditions. "They said it was the coldest winter in forty years in France, and I believe them," remarked Biow. "It was misery." Private Ned

Ghost Army soldiers in Briey

Harris acquired a potbellied stove that he installed in the back of his truck. It kept him and his buddies warm until an angry officer told them it was against regulations and forced them to get rid of it: "We went back to our cold feet." Lieutenant Bob Conrad recalled frequently being "on the ground, in snow, without a tent, and with mud around us.

SERVICE CLUB
PINE CAMP, N.Y.

"Premonition"

"Everything was packed. We were ready to move. Here we waited in Belgium, in a barrack, dilapidated by time and war, to go ahead. All were set just waiting for the word to move and we each wondered "Why? and Where?."

My Sleeping Bag by Walter Arnett, 1944

But we were still a hell of a lot luckier than the infantry. When we were moving in our vehicles, seeing our infantrymen slogging through on their feet, with the rain and snow coming down and walking in the mud, it made me thank whatever gods there may be that I had a vehicle."

In between their forays to the front, they were billeted in a gloomy old military barracks in Briey, France. The artists in the 603rd created an attic gallery to display the best of their work. They put on shows with titles like *Spontaneous Expressions* and *On Our Own Time*. It was both a diversion from the war and a way to share work normally hidden away in sketchbooks and backpacks.

Certain artists just naturally stood out. Private Arthur Singer's work with watercolors deeply impressed his fellow officers. Harris stood in awe of his technique: "I couldn't get a better teacher than Arthur." If they were in a billet for a week or more, Corporal John Jarvie recalled, Singer would decorate the walls by his bunk with birds and animals, "and he never penciled it in. He just took his brushes and painted

Art exhibits at the attic gallery in Briey, France

it." Sergeant Keith Williams was admired for his etchings, Private First Class Belisario Contreras for his work with pen and ink. Contreras "was a master at the art of taking lines, putting them together, and making visual sense out of them," said Ned Harris. Sergeant George Vander Sluis was another artist deeply respected by his peers. "Very urbane, very elegant," recalled Corporal Jack Masey. Private Harold Dahl actually dug into his pocket to buy some of Vander Sluis's work. In letters home he also raved about the sketches and paintings done by his friend Private First Class Cleo Hovel.

(top) *To My Friend Belisario, Who Should Have Known Better* by Keith Williams, 1945

(bottom) *Self-Portrait* by Arthur Singer, 1945

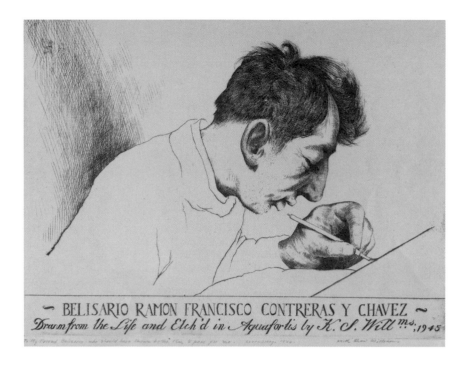

Bill Blass in his jeep

The cover and one page from one of Bill Blass's wartime sketchbooks

One of the most memorable Ghost Army artists was Private First Class Bill Blass. Originally from Indiana, Blass moved to New York at age seventeen to pursue a career in fashion design. His fellow soldiers took to him immediately. "A fine fellow in every sense of the word," wrote Harold Dahl in a letter home. "Very flamboyant, very outgoing, very cheerful," said Sergeant Bob Tompkins, who was close friends with Blass during the war. "He would never shirk a duty," recalled Private William Sayles. "If it was cleaning trash cans, he was right there with a smile and beautiful teeth." In his autobiography, *Bare Blass*, written with *New York Times* fashion reporter Cathy Horyn, Blass admitted he was in a "bubble of delight" during the war. "For me, the three and a half years that I spent in the army represented absolute freedom. I was truly on my own for the first time in my life. So, naturally, in that exuberant state of mind, I didn't always notice how bad things were."

Jack Masey remembered Blass reading *Vogue* in his foxhole. "The rest of us are a bunch of slobs, but not Blass—he's always dressed to the nines. We all had the same uniforms, but leave it to Blass to have his pressed or something." Certainly, outside of his army duties, his focus was almost entirely on fashion. He filled his notebooks with ideas for women's clothing. In Paris, Luxembourg, and elsewhere, when he saw an outfit he liked, it went down in the notebook. On the cover of one notebook he drew the mirror image *B*s that would become the logo for his fashion-design house.

No matter how cold or how depressing things got, the soldiers found stolen moments to gain some relief through "the wonder of art," as Ned Harris called it. "Sit down and immerse yourself in creating images, and you really go into another space. And it was that space that I think really helped us all."

John Jarvie recalled one night on guard duty in the Belgian town of Habay-la-Vieille. It was bitter cold, and as he huddled for warmth, he saw his buddy Keith Williams standing on guard some distance away, with his hands cupped in front of him. Jarvie asked him later what he had been doing, and Williams told him he had been painting

(left) *Sentry* by George Vander Sluis, 1945

(right) *Habay-la-Vieille* by John Jarvie, 1945

Waiting Their Turn by Ned Harris, 1945

a watercolor. "With what?" Jarvie asked, incredulous that he would take out a set of paints on guard duty. "He took out his watch, and he had a watch fob. The watch fob was made up of three little watercolor buttons. And his brush was the ferrule end of a watercolor brush with just the hairs. He did a beautiful watercolor with those three colors." Jarvie went back the next day and painted the same scene.

On another occasion, Harris and Jarvie made their way into the crowded brothel in nearby Homécourt. "It was a mob scene," remembered Harris. "The cruddiest-looking place you could imagine: filthy, noisy, and the absolute opposite from *amour.*" Rather than go upstairs with one of the French girls, the two artists set about capturing the scene in their sketchbooks. Combat engineers from the 406th, visiting the brothel with a different goal in mind, couldn't quite believe it. "They said, 'What are you doing here, sketching pictures?'"

One of Jarvie's sketches shows a soldier propositioning the madam. "But he couldn't afford her." Another captures a soldier combing his hair so he'll look his best. There's humor in the drawings, tinged with a sense of desperation. For many of the women, prostitution was the only way to feed their families as winter settled on war-ravaged France. "When they left at night," said Jarvie, "their husbands would wait outside the door for them and take them home."

    January 26, 1945
      I've seen some pretty miserable guys and also people who
    in this weather are forced to evacuate their homes with
    what they can carry on their backs, leaving their homes to
    be at the mercy of cold-hearted armies to whom a house is
    just a place where an enemy can hide. These people around
    here will wash all your laundry for an unbelievably small
    speck of food and walk 6 kilometers to deliver it.
    — Letter written by Harold Dahl

In later years, many Ghost Army veterans would emphasize how easy they had it compared to the frontline soldiers who were, in the military parlance, "at the sharp end of the stick." An incident in early March 1945 brought that home with stunning force. Trucks and drivers from the Twenty-Third were pressed into temporary service to ferry replacement troops to the front, near the German city of Saarlautern (now Saarlouis). Private Ellsworth Kelly was assigned to be one of the drivers. So was Ed Biow. "We picked up this division," he recalled. "Raw troops. Had never been in combat. Hadn't even had barely time to zero in their rifles." Some of the soldiers told Private Irving Stempel they

*Young Soldiers Being
Transported to the Front,
Remagen, Courtyard, Chateau
de Divonne, France by
Ellsworth Kelly, 1945*

had been in New York City just two weeks before. Biow remembered jamming them in so he could close the strap that went over the tailgate: "They were scared to pieces."

They brought the men up at night, under fire. "We sat there, bumper to bumper, and the Germans are firing what they called 'screaming meemies,' which were essentially rockets but designed to make a horrible screaming noise. And there you are, sitting there in the dark, bumper to bumper, no place to go, no way to hide, while these suckers are swinging over your head and making this awful noise." Machine guns chattered nearby. The young draftees, some sick to their stomach with fear, arrived at the front just in time to be thrown into a dawn attack across pontoon bridges.

What happened next remained seared into their memories. "They started over the bridges, the flares go off, and the Germans wipe them out," recalled Ed Biow. "One minute, there's a live guy in the back of your truck, and the next minute, he's laying dead out on a pontoon bridge somewhere." Both Kelly and Shilstone made haunting sketches of the untrained soldiers headed to their deaths. All of the Ghost Army soldiers involved were angered and distressed at the senseless deaths. "These young kids were just cannon fodder," said Bob Tompkins, more than sixty-five years later. "And that really upset a lot of us."

They knew, of course, that the same could happen to them. Increasingly, their missions were putting them in harm's way. Each action seemed to draw more and more artillery and mortar fire. So far they had taken few casualties, but the longer the war went on, the less the chance they could escape unscathed. And they could not shake the thought that the peculiar nature of their unit left them especially vulnerable. "If the Germans had known who we were and what we did, they could have just walked through," remarked Arthur Shilstone. "We had nothing really to protect ourselves. We had fifty-caliber machine guns on some of the trucks, our own personal arms, and that was it."

On March 12, 1945, the odds finally caught up with them.

The mission was called Operation Bouzonville. They were impersonating the Eightieth Infantry Division, pretending to prepare for an attack near Saarlautern in order to decoy Germans away from a real attack being planned farther north. By this time, they had it down to a science. Dummy artillery emplacements went up overnight. Sonic and radio played their shows. This was one of their shortest deceptions of the war, just thirty-three hours, and it went off without a hitch until the final moments.

As the deceivers were getting ready to move out, German artillery opened up on them. Private Harold Laynor was standing by one of the trucks when there was "a shattering, smashing, blinding series of explosions around us." The ground shook and heaved under their feet. Sergeant Victor Dowd was sitting in a truck full of soldiers with his driver when "a shell landed in front of us, and then a shell flew over our heads and hit the truck behind us. And I was thinking, 'Do I tell them to get the hell out of here now?' And with that, the signal came, and we moved. And it was just a case of luck," Dowd recalled years later. "*Luck*

Not Me Please by Harold Laynor, 1947

Medics and soldiers near Briey

is the paramount word. If you're in the wrong place, you can be dead. If you're in the right place, you can live to be as old as I am."

Sergeant George Peddle, a six-foot collegian from Philadelphia serving in the radio company, was riddled with shrapnel when his truck was hit. Private First Class William Anderson recalled that men went to help, but Peddle told them "Don't bother, I'm going to die," which he did, shortly thereafter. Fifteen more men were wounded, some quite severely. Private Joe Spence saw "people no more than twenty or thirty feet away from me who lost limbs because of shrapnel just falling all over." Captain Thomas Wells of the headquarters company was killed not far away when his jeep was caught in a different artillery barrage. It was the Ghost Army's deadliest operation. "This has really been a hell of a blow to us all," wrote Bob Tompkins in his diary. Like many soldiers in similar circumstances, he said a little prayer giving thanks that he was not one of those whose number had been called that day.

Harold Laynor, who said a similar prayer in the moment before the shells came down—*Not me, Lord*—was thrown against one of the trucks by the force of the explosion, a hunk of shrapnel embedded in his back. It soon became infected. Flown back to Paris for treatment, he was recuperating in a Paris hospital when painter Pablo Picasso visited the ward. Struck by Laynor's interest in his work, Picasso invited the young artist to visit him in his studio. "I found Picasso wonderful and it's not difficult to see why he is the top figure in the art world today," wrote Laynor to his wife, Gloria. "My visit to his studio and working with him greatly inspires me to continue with my painting." Laynor later said that Picasso exerted a major influence on his painting style. He was one soldier for whom the terrible day in March had a silver lining.

They knew they had been fortunate, that their losses had been light. "That kind of thing could have happened many more times than it did," remarked Dowd. But he and the others were sobered by it. Deception could be just as deadly as any other occupation in the war. "We could no longer say, 'What in the hell are we doing here? Nobody's shooting at us.'"

Just two weeks later, the men of the Ghost Army set out on what was to be their last and most important mission of the war.

Briey

In 1940 the French village of Briey was annexed by Germany, along with the rest of the Alsace-Lorraine region, and its resources were exploited for the German war machine. After Briey's liberation, the Ghost Army was based in a *caserne* (army barracks) there for a couple of months in early 1945.

Briey, March '45 by Bob Tompkins, 1945

Briey, 1945 by Ellsworth Kelly,
1945

Briey by Arthur Singer, 1945

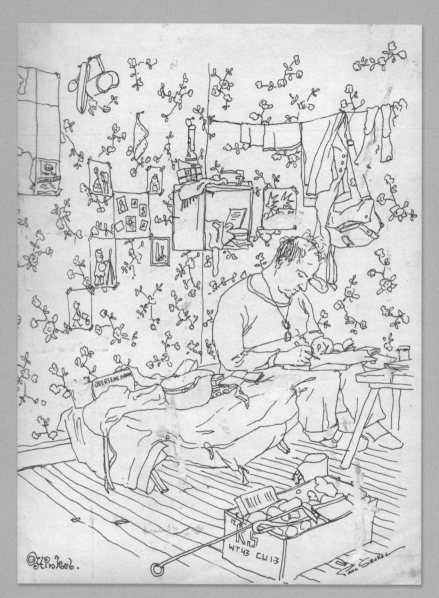

(left) *George Martin* by Paul
Seckel, 1945

(right) George Martin in his
room in Briey

Briey, France '45 by Joseph
Spence, 1945

A bombed street in Germany, photographed by Ghost Army soldier Irving Mayer, 1945

13

ONE LAST GRAND DECEPTION

Eleven hundred men, with help from a few regular army units, would try to convince the enemy that they were thirty thousand soldiers bristling for an all-out charge across the Rhine.

A fter nine months of bitter fighting, the war in Europe was nearly over. But there remained one last barrier for the Allied forces to cross: the Rhine River, the western boundary of Germany's industrial heartland. It was here that Allied generals expected the battered remnants of Hitler's once-proud army to mount their final defense of the fatherland.

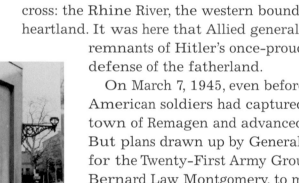

Dülken, Germany, 1945

(opposite) Map created in 1945 depicting Operation Viersen

On March 7, 1945, even before Operation Bouzonville, American soldiers had captured a bridge near the German town of Remagen and advanced some forces across the river. But plans drawn up by General Dwight D. Eisenhower called for the Twenty-First Army Group, under British General Bernard Law Montgomery, to make the major thrust across the Rhine. Two infantry divisions of the American Ninth Army, the Thirtieth and the Seventy-Ninth, would lead one wing of the attack, scheduled for March 24.

For Operation Viersen, the Ghost Army would work to fool the Germans into thinking that those two divisions were going to attack ten miles to the south. Pulling off this final performance would require them to operate on a bigger scale than ever, with potentially thousands of lives depending on them. "We moved on up to this last grand deception," as Private Ed Biow put it. The detailed plan was largely the work of Lieutenant Colonel Merrick Truly, one of the Twenty-Third's staff officers. Eleven hundred men, with help from a few regular army units, would try to convince the enemy that they were thirty thousand soldiers bristling for an all-out charge across the Rhine. No effort would be spared.

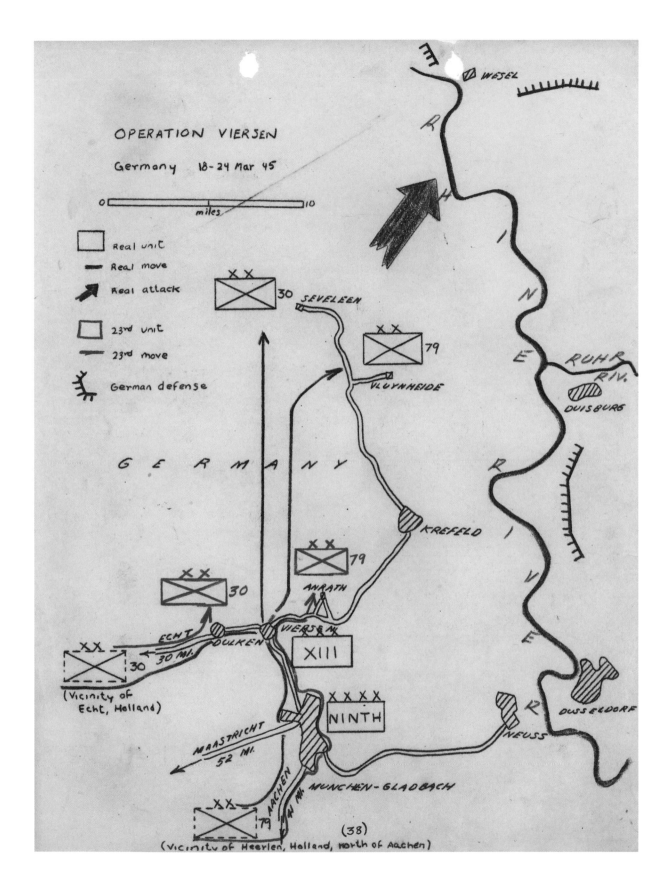

OPERATION VIERSEN

Germany   18-24 Mar 45

0 |——————————————| 10
miles

□ Real unit
▬ Real move
➤ Real attack
▢ 23rd unit
— 23rd move
⌇ German defense

WESEL

RHINE RIVER

RUHR RIV.

DUISBURG

GERMANY

30   SEVELEEN

79

VLUYNHEIDE

KREFELD

79

ANRATH

30

ECHT   VIERSEN
POULKEN   XIII

XX
30   30 MI.

(Vicinity of
Echt, Holland)

MAASTRICHT
52 MI.

NINTH

NEUSS

DUSSELDORF

AACHEN
34 MI.

MUNCHEN-GLADBACH

79

(Vicinity of Heerlen, Holland, North of Aachen)

(38)

TRAFFIC CONTROL NET SCRIPT
(taken from NCS radio log
18-25 March, 1945)

18 March

1907	From 6	(Readability OK except for interference).
1910	From 7	(3x3).
1915	From 9	(5x5).
1920	From 7	(Reported alternate channel clear, suggested we switch).
1925	To 6	(Asked him to contact 2. He was unable to do so).
1950	From 6	POINT OF C130 PASSED AT 1925.
1952	From 7	POINT OF C126 PASSED AT 1955.
2002	From 7	C126 MOVING UP EAST BETWEEN HERE AND BOISHEM MOVING SLOWLY.
2022	From 6	DELAY BETWEEN SERIALS NEXT ONE SIGHTED.
2037	To 9	THERE ARE GUIDES AT DULKEN TO DIRECT C130 THROUGH VIERSEN.
2044	To 7	(Asked him to contact 2).
2055	From 6	MOVEMENT BETWEEN SERIALS VERY SPOTTY.
2103	To 6	WATCH SECURITY.
2108	From 9	(Inquired as to contact with 2. We have not been able to contact 2).
2122	CQ	SEE LONG FORM DICKEY WANTS COMPLETE 3A AT YOUR STATION STARTING 191100 STOP 191300.
2140	From 7	ONE COLUMN TURNED LEFT N221 REROUTED ONTO L212 EAST.
2207	From 7	TELL ENGLISH HIS PROMOTION CAME THROUGH.
2222	To 9	SIX SAW POINT C130 AT 1925. WHEN DID IT PASS YOU?
2228	From 6	GROUP MISSED L31 RHEINDAHLEN. PUT THEM ON N59.
2236	To 9	KEEP US POSTED ON TIMES.
2244	From 7	BIG BREAK IN COLUMN.

- 1 -

Incl No 15

Stanley Nance named his radio jeep Kilowatt Kommand and flew this pennant from the antenna.

As the real divisions were moving into the north, their radio operators went off the air at a preassigned moment. Ghost Army radio operators began imitating them, creating the illusion that the troops were traveling to the point of the fake attack. Sergeant Stanley Nance transmitted thirty messages from eight different locations to simulate the movement toward the front. He took pains to match the power of his transmitter to the power of the one he was replacing. Lacking sophisticated measuring equipment, he used a simple expedient: he held a pencil close to the antenna of the division's powerful radio set to see how big a spark he could generate between the pencil and the antenna. Then he dialed up his own power to achieve the same spark.

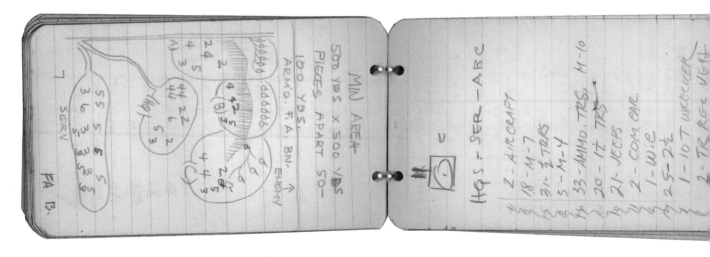

Tony Young's notebook shows the standard plan for the bivouac of an armored division. This was used to make the deceptions more accurate.

(opposite) Deceptive radio script used during Operation Viersen

Camoufleurs laid down smoke screens at the Rhine, near the town of Krefeld, as if they were trying to hide a build-up there. They set up fake supply dumps and staffed phony headquarters. This close to the Rhine, the Germans were putting up every airplane they could to spot what the Americans were doing. The Twenty-Third responded by inflating more than two hundred decoy vehicles around the towns of Anrath and Dülken to create the illusion of a massive military presence a few miles west of the river. Dummy trucks and tanks were parked in forests, courtyards, and open fields. Real armored vehicles and infantry were used to enhance the illusion. A handful of antiaircraft gun emplacements were beefed up with eighty dummy guns.

Dummy tanks, phony
command post, and fake
supply depot set up for
Operation Viersen

Inflated rubber airplane

March 22, 1945
    Checked items and then chow. Slept in farmhouse for 2 1/2 hours.... Have more dummies up now than we've ever had before. Not permitted to speak to civilians. White flags on every door. Feeling very lonesome and homesick tonight.
— Diary of Sergeant Bob Tompkins

Each army division in World War II was equipped with a few small planes able to take off from simple grass airfields to conduct air observation or emergency transportation. The men of the Twenty-Third laid out a phony airfield for each of the divisions they were impersonating and set up inflatable L-5 observation planes. So convincing were the phony airfields that a real observation plane mistakenly landed at one— and was promptly told to get lost.

The sonic company worked around the clock. At night they played the sounds of trucks rolling in. In the daytime they set up near a lake a few miles to the rear and played sounds of bridge construction, to suggest that engineers were practicing building the pontoon bridges that would be used to cross the Rhine after an initial attack. Actual bridging units were attached to the Twenty-Third and assembled some real bridge sections to give credibility to the illusion.

Aerial view of dummies set up at Anrath-Dülken

The lesson of coordination, in such short supply at Brest, had been well learned. A battalion of infantry was attached to each notional division for verisimilitude. The Ninth Army flew real reconnaissance missions over the zone of the fake attack and stepped up artillery attacks from that area. The placement of army hospitals also suggested the attack would come there.

On the eve of the Rhine crossing, Supreme Allied Commander Dwight D. Eisenhower and British Prime Minister Winston Churchill joined General Bernard Law Montgomery to witness the momentous occasion. Tremendous effort had gone into the deception. But no one knew whether it would really work.

In the early morning hours of March 24, navy landing craft began crossing the Rhine. Infantrymen on board steeled themselves for fierce fighting. What they found instead was weak and disorganized resistance, as if the Germans were expecting the attack someplace else. Thirty-one GIs were killed in the crossing. "The Ninth US Army [got] across with so few casualties," says Roy Eichhorn, former director of research and development at the United States Army Combined Arms Center, "they would almost have [had] that many casualties if they [had been] running a big training exercise."

United States Army intelligence officers were convinced that the deception had made it possible.

> The real troops engaged in the Rhine Crossing were
> delighted with the success of the cover operation. The
> 30th G-2 [Intelligence Officer] said the United States
> attack came as a "complete surprise to the enemy with a
> consequent saving of American lives." The 79th G-2 captured
> a German overlay [map] of the American Order of Battle just
> prior to the attack. It had the 79th placed approximately
> where the Twenty-third had portrayed it and had lost the
> 30th altogether. The NINTH ARMY G-2 stated that the Germans
> expected the main allied effort to be made north of Wesel
> with a minor crossing opposite Krefeld. "There is no
> doubt," he said "that Operation VIERSEN materially assisted
> in deceiving the enemy with regard to the real dispositions
> and intentions of this Army."
> — Official History of the 23rd Headquarters Special Troops

Lieutenant John Walker was one of many Ghost Army soldiers who felt immense pride that they managed to pull off such a large illusion. "You go up against the best army there is, the best group of soldiers, and you dupe them successfully, you pat yourself on the back."

> March 24, 1945
>   Generals who viewed our stuff from the air yesterday
> claimed a great deal of credit for this deceptive move
> goes to us. Jerry must have copped it all with his camera
> the past couple of days. XIII Corps really thinks we're
> hot stuff.
> — Diary of Sergeant Bob Tompkins

"We were told we spent three years in the army just for that one week," said Private Edward Boccia years later, recalling how successful the operation was deemed to be. "In some people's minds," says Roy

(opposite) Letter of
commendation for the
Twenty-Third Headquarters
Special Troops

Eichhorn, "it probably justifies the existence of the whole unit. And it's pretty impressive." One of those impressed was the Commander of the Ninth Army, General William Simpson. He wrote a letter of commendation calling the deception "an important part of the operation," adding that it reflected "great credit on this unit."

Private Harold Dahl was understandably excited about the commendation when he wrote home about it a few weeks later, after censorship had been lifted. "We understand he also recommended us for a Presidential Citation," he boasted. "We are mighty proud of that little deal." The presidential unit citation never happened. But Simpson's letter, one of the only pieces of official recognition they received during the war, was praise aplenty: a glowing review for the final performance of the Ghost Army.

Sign near Dülken,
Germany 1945

HEADQUARTERS
NINTH UNITED STATES ARMY
Office of the Commanding General

APO
29 March 1945

SUBJECT: Commendation

TO : Commanding Officer, 23d Headquarters Special Troops, Twelfth Army Group.
THRU: Commanding General, Twelfth Army Group

1. 23d Headquarters Special Troops, Twelfth Army Group, was attached to NINTH UNITED STATES ARMY on 15 March 1945 to participate in the operation to cross the RHINE River.

2. The unit was engaged in a special project, which was an important part of the operation. The careful planning, minute attention to detail, and diligent execution of the tasks to be accomplished by the personnel of the organization reflect great credit on this unit.

3. I desire to commend the officers and men of the 23d Headquarters Special Troops, Twelfth Army Group, for their fine work and to express my appreciation for a job well done.

RECEIVED
1 APR 1945
AG - MAIL SECTION
HQ TWELFTH ARMY GROUP

MAILED
31 MAR 1945
HQ
9th ARMY

/s/ W. H. Simpson
/s/T/ W. H. SIMPSON,
Lieutenant General, U. S. Army,
Commanding.

The USS General O. H. Ernst

14

A TOAST TO FREEDOM

Now, if you've been in the darkness for all that time,
and your lights are going on, that's spectacular. And the city
was mobbed. The town square, you didn't see anybody
until the lights went on, and suddenly you realize there's
thousands of people here. What a feeling! All the blinds
in the houses opened. The streetlights went on, people cheered,
they carried torches. It was absolutely thrilling to see.

— John Jarvie

Trier is one of the oldest cities in Germany, established by the Romans more than two thousand years ago. A Roman bridge constructed in the second century carries commuters across the Moselle River to this day. But in April 1945 the city was in ruins, having suffered devastating damage from Allied bombers. It was here that the Ghost Army came for the final stop on their long trek across Europe.

Despite the destruction, Trier retained a haunting beauty. Climbing the hills east of town, some of the Ghost Army artists painted the

Trier by Alvin Shaw, 1945

(opposite) *Trier* by Arthur Singer, 1945

203　**CHAPTER 14: A TOAST TO FREEDOM**

(top) *Germany 1945* by Ned
Harris, 1945

(bottom) *Bridge over
the Moselle* by Belisario
Contreras, 1945

(left) *Bill Blass* by Victor Dowd, 1945

(right) Making curfew signs at one of the camps. Clockwise from top left: William Sayles, Frank Geary, Bill Blass, Gil Switzer, and David Taffy

bombed-out bridges crossing the Moselle. (The Roman bridge had survived with only minor damage.) Their deception days were over. They had been sent to Trier to carry out one last mission that brought them face to face with Hitler's dirty work and brought home the reality of war. The men of the Twenty-Third Headquarters Special Troops were assigned to help guard five camps for displaced persons (known as DPs) in and around Trier.

By the end of the war, millions of people in Europe had been displaced from their homes. They included victims of the Holocaust, those who had fled the fighting, and huge numbers of people forced into slave labor by the Nazis. The camps now guarded by the Twenty-Third contained tens of thousands of refugees from all over Europe.

> These wretched people were officially called Displaced Persons but they were really liberated slaves of Nazi Germany. They needed food, shelter, clothes, baths, orientation and transport back to their native lands.... The DPs were divided into 26 foreign nationalities — many who hated each other — and all were feared and despised by the native Germans.
>
> — Official History of the 23rd Headquarters Special Troops

These were people who had been horribly mistreated by Hitler's regime, "and they had just gone crazy," recalled Sergeant Jack McGlynn. "One can hardly blame them. They were pillaging, they were killing people in town, and they had to be guarded so that they wouldn't kill more Germans." The assignment didn't sit well with many of the Ghost Army soldiers. Locking up the DPs (many of whom were from Allied nations) to protect the Germans (with whom they were officially still at war) seemed to have an Alice in Wonderland quality.

```
April 15, 1945
   Russians and Poles stealing everything they can get their
hands on, and I don't blame them. Resent having to guard a
goddamn Heinie. Some Russians are hiding in the hills with
guns and raiding the Germans at night. If we were smart
we'd turn our backs.
```
— Diary of Sergeant Bob Tompkins

Ghost Army soldiers were posted in pairs outside the barbed wire. Corporal John Jarvie witnessed many escape attempts. "You would hear

(left) *Breakout* by John Jarvie, 1945

(right and opposite) Displaced persons camps, Germany, 1945

the slightest jingle on the barbed wire and flash on a light, and you'd find some guy maybe five feet away from you, crawling at you. They didn't care if they killed you to get out or just beat the hell out of you... and you'd throw a burst of Tommy gun fire across—not to hit them, to push them back in."

One night, Sergeant Tompkins and other soldiers were assigned to sleep at a local estate to protect it from marauding DPs. Some mornings he had to ride shotgun on a German farmer's milk truck to prevent the farmer from being robbed as he went about his rounds.

On April 17 six Russians from the camp in Wittlich, Germany, entered a nearby village looking for flour. Angry townspeople attacked them and killed two of the Russians. The next day, soldiers from the Twenty-Third raided the village, bringing angry Russian DPs with them to identify the wrongdoers.

April 19, 1945
  Russians went first and when crowd came out with pitchforks, Jeeps with 50's [.50-caliber machine guns] closed in. Russians choked hell out of Heinies and Tony [Young] let loose with 50's to stop Heinies from running away.
— Diary of Sergeant Bob Tompkins

A villager with a pitchfork ran at Private Charles Boulliane but was tackled by a Russian DP. Six Germans were arrested. The refugees wanted the GIs to take more aggressive action in incidents of this sort. "They wonder why we don't shoot the Germans," wrote Bob Tompkins. "I wonder myself."

Displaced Persons

Many of the artists in the 603rd, moved by the character
and suffering they saw in the faces of the DPs, sketched
portraits of them. Sergeant Victor Dowd made dozens
in a single day. "It was a really interesting experience for a
young artist. I asked somebody to sit, and I did a five-minute
sketch, and the next thing I know there [were] three or four
people waiting to have their pictures drawn. Some
of the best drawings that I did are [of] these displaced
people, because they are drawings of arrogant young men,
tired-looking old men, haggard-looking women, young
women in costumes. They were fascinating and wonderful
for somebody who is interested in drawing people."

The refugees were eager to sit for a portrait.
"We would let them sign their names on the pictures,"
Private Ned Harris recalled. "They had lost everything,
so to them the simple act of having their portraits
drawn was to let the world know they were still alive.
It gave them back some of their dignity."

The Old Man by
Victor Dowd, 1945

*Joseph, Chudzik, Displaced
Polish Boy, Bitburg, Germany
by Ellsworth Kelly, 1945*

Portraits of three refugees
by Victor Dowd, 1945

(left) *A Comrade '45* by
Edward Boccia, 1945

(right) *Olga* by James Steg,
1945

Maria by Ned Harris, 1945

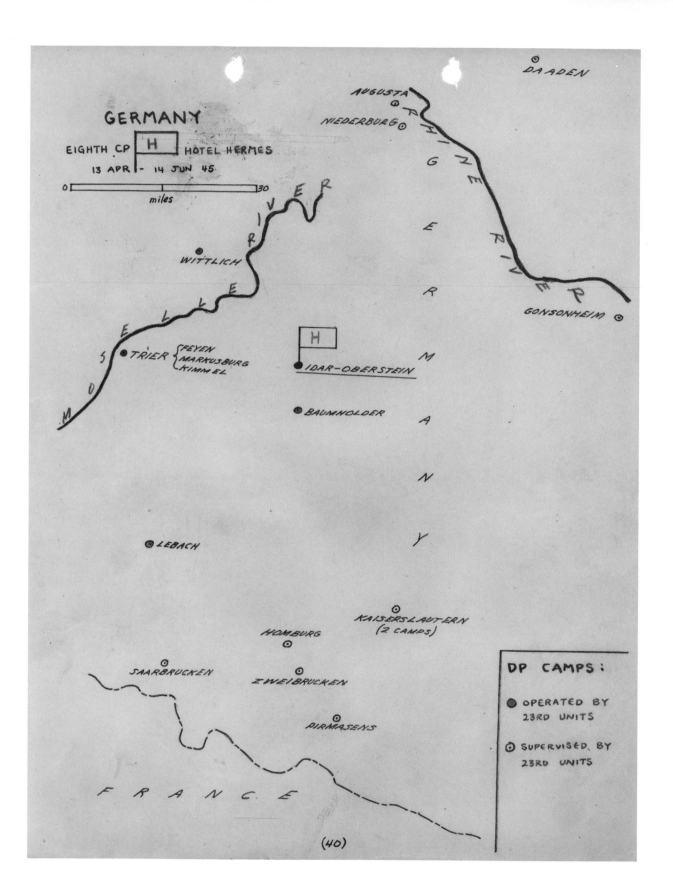

Sergeant Victor Dowd couldn't believe it when he got orders to lead a patrol into the countryside to round up another batch of Russian DPs who had escaped and were stealing food from villagers. "Talk about ludicrous. Now the army is going crazy. They want us to capture Russians because they are harassing Germans. Don't they remember that we were shooting at the Germans just a little while ago, and more importantly, they were killing us?" Searching through the woods, .45 in hand, Dowd came across a Russian whom he judged to be just about the same age as he was. The man surrendered voluntarily, "for which I'm very grateful, because I don't know how I would have handled the dilemma of having to shoot somebody whom I considered my ally."

On another such expedition, Private Buzz Senat did shoot two Russian teenagers who had been terrorizing German families in the vicinity. "These two kids were shot in this forest, lying on the floor like sacks of flour," recalled Corporal Jack Masey, "and we had to throw them on a truck. They were dead. I never quite recovered from that." Masey had just been through one of the most horrible wars in history. But perhaps because this incident happened when the war and the killing were all but over, this incident shook him up more than anything else that had happened. "I'm nineteen or twenty. Here they are. They're sixteen. What kind of blow is this? What kind of fate are we dealing with? Why am I the lucky one, and why are they the unlucky ones?"

Things were little better inside the barbed wire. Several of the camps contained both Russians and Poles. "They hated each other's guts," recalled Bob Tompkins, "and they were killing each other every night. And we were supposed to control things. And we'd had no experience in police matters, and so there was a lot of chaos at night." The Russian DPs used stolen potatoes to distill a powerful homemade vodka that fueled the problem. Food was in chronically short supply. Officers went into Trier and gave the mayor a list of foodstuffs required to feed the DPs. The next day they brought trucks down into town, but there was almost no food available. The mayor said the people in his town simply did not have any food to spare. Lieutenant Gil Seltzer remembered that one of the officers told the mayor that if the food wasn't there the next day, the Americans would open the gates of the camp and let the DPs loose upon the city. By the following morning, all the requested food had been supplied. Eventually the army started trucking in rations.

One of the goals of the Allied forces was to repatriate the displaced people to their homelands. But many of the Russians did not want to go. "A lot were fearful of returning," said Victor Dowd. "Maybe they knew more than we did about what lay in store for them." Jack Masey had the unpleasant duty of getting the Russian refugees to board trains that would take them back to Moscow. "We noticed that they didn't want to get on these trains. 'You're going home—aren't you happy?' 'No, we don't want to go home.'" The DPs had heard rumors, which turned out to be all too true, about the circumstances that likely awaited them. Joseph Stalin's paranoia led the Soviet dictator to suspect all Russian soldiers and civilians captured by the Germans of being collaborators. (He had his own daughter-in-law arrested when his son was captured by the Germans.) Those who headed back would most likely face harsh interrogation, imprisonment in the Gulag, or execution. They didn't want to go. "And these were families, maybe a husband and wife and kid, not wanting to get on these trains," recalled Masey with some anguish. "We forced them on the trains."

Their assignment guarding the DP camps extended into early May. By this time the Russians had been separated from the Poles. A Soviet army officer who had arrived on the scene encouraged the DPs to stage a May Day parade with banners and singing. Several Ghost Army officers, including Lieutenant Fred Fox, stood on a reviewing platform featuring a large picture of Stalin. Smiles seemed to be missing all around.

Life in Germany wasn't too hard for the men of the Ghost Army. Like American soldiers all across occupied territory, they turned people out of their houses and took them over for themselves. "I'm getting

May Day parade at DP camp

(top) *Wittlich, Germany* by
William Sayles, 1945

(bottom) *Peeling Potatoes with
Two Russian Girls* by Victor
Dowd, 1945

to be quite a German," Private Harold Dahl wrote home. "Sitting on a German bed, writing a letter by the light of a German candle, in German ink, with a German geography as a board, while German rhubarb cooks on our little stove and we have German music piped in thru a German telephone."

Every platoon was given a house, recalled William Sayles, set on a pristine quarter of an acre of land. His house "was gorgeous, like a dollhouse, everything perfect." Upstairs, Sayles found documents showing that the family who owned the house had lost three sons in the war, which saddened him. In a cupboard he found a little souvenir pitcher with a picture of his hometown, Albany, New York, painted on it, an uncanny coincidence. A sergeant in Sayles's platoon ordered his men to dig up the backyard, guessing that's where the owners would hide their food and valuables. They found their buried treasures: sacks of potatoes and crocks of butter, along with a few fur coats. "We did nothing but make french fries, day and night!" marveled Sayles.

The DP camps were not too far from Luxembourg City, and the soldiers occasionally had a chance to visit. John Jarvie recalled being there when the lights officially came back on after years of wartime blackout:

```
Now, if you've been in the darkness for all that time,
and your lights are going on, that's spectacular. And the
city was mobbed. The town square, you didn't see anybody
until the lights went on, and suddenly you realize there's
thousands of people here. What a feeling! All the blinds
in the houses opened. The streetlights went on, people
cheered, they carried torches. It was absolutely thrilling
to see.
```

Back in Germany, another one of the artists in the 603rd, Sergeant Stanley Wright, commandeered an attic that he and others used as a studio. On May 8, 1945, they were painting a girl named Janina "with a wonderful radiance in her eyes," as Wright wrote home that night to his mother.

The Studio by William Sayles, 1945

(opposite) Discharge papers for Ghost Army soldier Marion Pastorcich

```
We all sipped wine as we worked
and we worked hard and fast as
the beautiful ball of fire was
quickly slipping behind the
purple hills. Then on the outside
voices, at first like a murmur
and then in the form of shouts,
told us that at long last it
was over. The voices were muffled
but we sensed the meaning - a
rush to the windows, let out
a burst - an inner prayer, a toast to freedom - then back
to painting for another hour before dusk engulfed us all.
Back home I can imagine the joy, the celebrating, the
enthusiasm - but to most of the boys over here a moment to
relax, an unbelievable calm with a chance to let the mind
slip back a year or so and wonder if it was all a dream -
[or] nightmare.
```

Hitler was one week in the grave, and German generals had surrendered to General Dwight D. Eisenhower the previous day in Reims, France. The fighting in Europe was officially done. Everyone celebrated. "It's a beautiful world tonight," Bob Tompkins wrote in his diary. "It's been a long hard road and we thank god it's over."

SEPARATION QUALIFICATION RECORD

SAVE THIS FORM. IT WILL NOT BE REPLACED IF LOST

This record of job assignments and special training received in the Army is furnished to the soldier when he leaves the service. In its preparation, information is taken from available Army records and supplemented by personal interview. The information about civilian education and work experience is based on the individual's own statements. The veteran may present this document to former employers, prospective employers, representatives of schools or colleges, or use it in any other way that may prove beneficial to him.

1. LAST NAME—FIRST NAME—MIDDLE INITIAL			MILITARY OCCUPATIONAL ASSIGNMENTS		
PASTORCICH, MARION			10. MONTHS	11. GRADE	12. MILITARY OCCUPATIONAL SPECIALTY
2. ARMY SERIAL No.	3. GRADE	4. SOCIAL SECURITY No.	3	Pvt	Engineer Basic (729)
15 322 317 See Honorable 8	Pfc	Unknown	34	Pfc	Camoufleur (804)
5. PERMANENT MAILING ADDRESS (Street, City, County, State)					
1221 Addison Avenue, Cleveland, Cuyahoga County, Ohio					
6. DATE OF ENTRY INTO ACTIVE SERVICE	7. DATE OF SEPARATION	8. DATE OF BIRTH			
21 Sep 1942	20 Oct 1945	8 Dec 1921			
9. PLACE OF SEPARATION					
Separation Point Camp Sibert, Alabama					

SUMMARY OF MILITARY OCCUPATIONS

13. TITLE—DESCRIPTION—RELATED CIVILIAN OCCUPATION

CAMOUFLEUR: As a member of 603rd Engineer Camouflage Battalion trained in the United States and in combat conducted a campaign of deception against the enemy. In five (5) campaigns, used dummy tanks, vehicles and guns to deceive enemy as to strength of Allied Troops and deployment of same. Drove light vehicles on which these dummies were mounted; also chauffeured officer in charge of platoon. Possessed a high degree of color discrimination and blended paints to produce natural effects. Understood effects of changing weather conditions on camouflage.

WD AGO FORM 100
1 JUL 1945

This form supersedes WD AGO Form 10), 15 July 1944, which will not be used.

The Commanding Officer of Troops on this ship is
Col. Harry L. Reeder, CO of the 23rd Headquarters,
Special Troops. This is the story of his command.

The 23rd Hq Sp Trps has probably been associated with more Armies and been
to more places than any other unit aboard ship. Some of its members landed
on D-day with the First Army. Later part of the command participated in the
Brittany campaign with the Third Army. When Field Marshall Montgomery crossed
the Rhine in March the 23rd was attached to the Ninth Army. Finally, when
the war was practically over, this versatile outfit took charge of 100,000
milling Displaced Persons for the Fifteenth Army.

The itinerary of the 23rd sounds like a roll call of famous place names,
altho modest members of this unit will be the first to admit that they
were not entirely responsible for publicizing these once-quiet little
towns. They watched the liberation of Cherbourg, drove thru the rubble
of St. Lo, could have been cut off by the German counter-attack at Mor-
tain, helped put the squeeze on Von Ramcke at Brest, took the cheers and
kisses of frenzied Parisions, were second into Luxembourg after the 5th
Armored Division, shared the cold snows south of Bastogne with the 4th
Armored Division (but don't let any 23rder tell you he relieved the
101st Airborne!), hung around the dreary Saarland with XX Corps, gaped
as the 17th A/B flew over to secure a bridgehead on the lower Rhine.
One detachment got as far as Pollwitz, a few miles from Czechoslovakia.

Almost any man in this peripatetic unit can toast in six different languages,
and talk knowingly of the ETO campaign from the beaches to the Elbe.

Naturally, there have been some exciting moments. For instance, last summer
one column was temporarily mislaid near Lorient; or when on 16 Dec the cooks
and KP's of the 4th Infantry Division held the Germans just east of Luxembourg's 23rd Hq; or when the Displaced Persons rioted at Trier because one
nationality thought another nationality was borrowing its water while actually stealing its women.

After a month or so mouthing such sweet place names as Boston, New York, Den-
ver, Phoenix and Kalamazoo, the 23rd Hq Sp Trps will possibly down a series
of Oriental sourballs including Chofu, Uchidonari, Tonigusuku, Hakonegasaki
and Fuchu. Igaga desu ka!

FAREWELL AND GOOD LUCK

Since there will be no Sunday edition of ERNST EVENTS, this will be the final edition for the current voyage. Therefore, it is with extreme sincerity that
we of the U.S.S. GENERAL O. H. ERNST bid all of you fellows (yes, and you two
excellent examples of fine American womanhood – the Red Cross workers, too) farewell and good luck. We have felt honored at being placed in contact with you
who have done so much to bring this dreadful conflict to a successful conclusion.

During the almost twelve months this vessel has been in commission we have come
in contact with a varied assortment of personnel, both service and civilian. In
most cases they all lived up to the high standards demanded of such personnel.
But no group surpassed the passenger personnel on board during the current trip.
You have all behaved as ladies and gentlemen and have left nothing but the finest
of cordial feelings with those of us who will remain aboard to transport still
more passengers to various places throughout the world. Possibly we will some day
have the pleasure of meeting some of you again. But whatever the fates hold in
store, for now we can simply say to all of you – FAREWELL AND GOOD LUCK.

On June 23, 1945, the USS *General O. H. Ernst* transport ship lifted anchor from Le Havre, carrying home, among others, the men of the Ghost Army. "The voyage was smooth, the quarters clean, the prospect glorious," noted the unit's official history. The ship arrived in Norfolk, Virginia, on July 2, and the men were given thirty days' leave. Bob Tompkins reunited with his wife three days later, on July 5. "Wellllllll—you know the rest!!!!!!!!!" he wrote in his diary, the final entry. "It was the most wonderful moment in my life."

> The day I got out of the army, I think, was the happiest day of my life. It wasn't the day that I got married, or when my first son was born, or anything else. It was when I got out of the army.
>
> — Corporal Arthur Shilstone

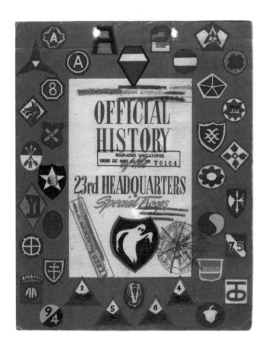

Official History of the 23rd Headquarters Special Troops by Fred Fox

(opposite) On the way home, the shipboard paper, the *Ernst Enquirer*, printed a vague history of the Twenty-Third designed to both impress and obfuscate.

After their leave, the men gathered again to prepare for the invasion of Japan. But the atomic bombs dropped on August 6 and 9, and the announcement on August 15 that Japan was surrendering eliminated the need for that assault. Suddenly men who thought they were headed for Japan were headed for civilian life. The soldiers were let out of the army in order, according to a military point system.

As the war wound down, Fox, recently promoted to captain, was selected to write the official United States Army history of the unit. Fox joked that he got the job because he wrote such compelling citations for other people's medals and spent so much time writing letters to his fiancée, Hannah Putnam, back home. Whatever the reason, it is safe to say that the resulting document is probably one of the most entertaining unit histories ever written. It ends with these words:

> On 30 August, Army Ground Forces wrote SECOND ARMY that the Twenty-third was to be deactivated by 15 September. Its ashes were to be placed in a small Ming urn and eventually tossed into the China Sea.
>
> On 10 September the Twenty-third Adjutant told your 87-pointed historian that the only thing that kept him from being released was the completion of this story. So now it's done and tomorrow I will be a free man again.
>
> The End.
>
> Frederic E. Fox
>
> — Official History of the 23rd Headquarters Special Troops

EPILOGUE
LAUDABLE AND GLORIOUS

There are German records that show that some
of the deceptions were taken — hook, line and sinker.
The Twenty-Third did not win the war single-handedly,
but I think it would have cost a lot more
American casualties had they not been there.

— Jonathan Gawne, military historian

Though fraud in all other actions be odious, yet in matters
of war it is laudable and glorious, and he who overcomes
his enemies by stratagem is as much to be praised as he who
overcomes them by force.

— Niccolò Machiavelli, *Discourses on Livy*

W hat should be the final verdict on the Twenty-Third Headquarters
Special Troops accomplishments? Shortly after V-E Day, Colonel
Billy Harris and Major Ralph Ingersoll of the Twelfth Army Group's
Special Plans Branch (along with Captain Went Eldredge, who worked
with them) issued a secret report that offered both pros and cons. They
held up Operation Viersen as an exemplary success. "This action alone
provides sufficient evidence on the practicability of tactical deception in
battle." But they suggested that overall, the Ghost Army failed to achieve
all it could have. "Tactical deception, despite a record of successful minor
manipulations of enemy intelligence, was characterized by a succession
of wasted opportunities." Some other experts have echoed this negative
point of view, arguing that the unit's accomplishments were minimal.

But a chorus of voices offers substantial praise for the Twenty-Third.
Thirty years after the war, a United States Army analyst named Mark
Kronman wrote a classified report praising the unit. "Rarely, if ever, has
there been a group of such a few men which had so great an influence on
the outcome of a major military campaign." Roy Eichhorn, former director of research and development at the United States Army Combined
Arms Center, put it this way: "Did it baffle the Germans every time?
Probably not. Did it cause the Germans to react in ways that we wanted
them to react? Definitely." Military historian Jonathan Gawne is convinced that the unit's deceptions had a significant impact on the war.
"There are German records that show that some of the deceptions were
taken—hook, line and sinker. The Twenty-Third did not win the war
single-handedly, but I think it would have cost a lot more American
casualties had they not been there."

Surviving veterans have drawn their own conclusions. "You know you saved lives. You don't know how many you saved, but you know you saved them," commented John Jarvie. "They say we saved fifteen or thirty thousand lives with our maneuvers," noted Spike Berry, using a figure that was mentioned in army reports. "But even if we only saved fifteen or thirty, it was worth it." Not everyone who served in the Ghost Army was sure that their efforts had been meaningful. Corporal Jack Masey, for example, long wondered if anyone had noticed or believed in their deceptions. But all found themselves in agreement with the sentiments put forth by Stanley Nance:

```
Of all the radio messages that I sent, could there have
been just one of those that changed the tide of battle for
an American victory, where one mother or one new bride was
spared the agony of putting a Gold Star [honoring a fallen
family member] in their front window? That's what the
Twenty-Third Headquarters was all about.
```

The *Worcester Daily Telegram* got such a huge response to their August 1945 Ghost Army story that the newspaper reprinted it in October 1945.

In the summer of 1945, Sebastian Messina, a twenty-eight-year-old corporal from the Signal Company Special went home to Worcester, Massachusetts, for a few weeks' leave. While there, he talked to a newspaper reporter from the *Worcester Daily Telegram* about his unusual wartime experiences. The reporter wrote a story, which the paper duly submitted to War Department censors. The censors asked the *Telegram* to withhold it from publication. But two weeks after Emperor Hirohito announced the surrender of Japan, the paper felt free to go to press.

Messina's revelations led to the first telling of the Ghost Army tale. The front-page story that appeared on August 29, 1944, was remarkably complete, full of drama and detail. "Ghost Army Fools Foe in Neatest Trick of War," the headline read. Messina, quoted liberally in the story, came across as funny, articulate, and proud of what he and his fellow deceivers had done. "One slip might have meant our necks," he told the reporter. "They never caught on to us, never found out we existed, because we were always somebody else." Spike Berry just happened to be in Worcester that day, on leave visiting a family friend. He couldn't believe it when saw the

headline. "All the secrecy we had, and they had us on the front page of the *Worcester Daily Telegram*!" Several news services picked it up. A spate of other stories followed from October 1945 to February 1946, including articles in the *New York Times* and *Newsweek*.

Some veterans disparage Messina as the man who talked too soon and "blew the cover" on the unit because he "couldn't wait to be a local hero." But the issue of secrecy is a complicated one. Did the Army consider the numerous stories a security breach? No one in authority ever said it was. But of course saying so would have just drawn attention to the story.

During the war, there is no question that secrecy was paramount. "There wasn't a time I remember that they didn't drill us on secrecy," said Stanley Nance. "They kept hammering that at us all the time… that our life depended on how well we kept our secret." But once the war was over, did the secret need to be kept? Some men—especially officers, as well as those in the sonic unit—were cautioned not to talk about it. "Basically, we were told we couldn't tell our wives or anybody about what we did," said Corporal Al Albrecht. "It was totally secret."

(below and opposite) From the files of the United States Army: the paper trail on Fred Fox's 1949 and 1967 requests to declassify the story

FIRST CONGREGATIONAL CHURCH

WAUSEON, OHIO

Frederic Fox, Minister

WAR DEPT

~~DEAR~~
SIRS:

Can the story of the 23d Hq Sp Troops be released to the general public? During the war it had a Top Secret classification.

I was the unit historian for the 23d and would like to write a short article about it for the N.Y. Times.

Sincerely,

FREDERICK FOX

Capt. Sig. O (Ret) O-1634769

MEMO FOR RECORD

Some soldiers just assumed that secrecy was still in force. Others, such as Jack Masey, say no one ever told them to keep it secret. Interestingly, even some who didn't believe they were constrained to keep quiet didn't like to talk about it because they found it a bit embarrassing. "I was always concerned about talking about it," Bernie Mason said, "because it sounds so comical."

Whatever individual soldiers believed and whatever had been revealed to the newspapers, the Pentagon made significant efforts over the next four decades to keep the details of Ghost Army operations under wraps. Fred Fox was one of the first to encounter this. By 1949 Fox was an ordained minister for the First Congregational Church in Wauseon, Ohio. Itching to do some writing for a wider audience, he contacted the army to see if the top-secret story of the Ghost Army could now be told. He was informed that "much of the material is still confidential or secret." Fox turned to other topics instead. He became a prolific contributor to the *New York Times Magazine* and other publications, a "reverend reporter" in the words of his son. To mark the tenth anniversary of the Battle of the Bulge, he wrote an article that lightly touched on his unit's deception exploits without divulging too many details. His writing led to a stint as a White House aide to President Dwight D. Eisenhower.

Fox made another attempt to get the official history—which he himself had written—declassified in 1967. Now installed as Princeton University's recording secretary and made wise by his White House years to the ways of politics, he enlisted the help of former Secretary of the Army Stephen Ailes, Princeton '33, who had been elected to the university's board the year before. But even Ailes couldn't make much headway. The Army made it clear that the records, now at the National Archives, remained classified and were available only for "official research." Fox never got to publish a Ghost Army book, and the full story didn't come out until after his death.

Military historian Jonathan Gawne believes the rising tensions of the Cold War led the Pentagon to clamp down on the Ghost Army story. "When you have operations that work well against the Germans, you don't want to tell the Russians what you did, because then *they'll* be prepared for them, and it will be useless against them."

The Cold War was just starting to wind down in late 1984, when Arthur Shilstone brought up the topic of World War II over lunch with an editor and art director from *Smithsonian* magazine. They were amazed by his Ghost Army stories, and the lunchtime talk led to a 1985 *Smithsonian* article by Edwards Park, which Shilstone illustrated.

According to Roy Eichhorn, the army declassified the official history at one point, and then quickly reclassified it again. By the 1990s, however, it was completely out of the shadows.

Today, the men of the Ghost Army at long last are getting considerable public attention and recognition for their accomplishments.

In recognition of the Ghost Army's contribution to France during World War II, Ghost Army veteran A. B. Wilson of Slidell, Louisiana, was awarded France's highest decoration, a Legion of Honor, at the National WWII Museum, New Orleans, Louisiana, in September 2013.

Articles about the unit have appeared in newspapers and magazines all over the world. The United States Army has taken a renewed interest in its World War II deceivers and has started using the story to introduce a new generation of army officers to deception techniques. Best of all, this is happening while many of the veterans are still around to receive the plaudits they so richly deserve.

The Twenty-Third Headquarters Special Troops remains the only example of a mobile, multimedia, tactical deception unit in the history of the United States Army and perhaps in the history of war. The men in the unit demonstrated a special kind of bravery, frequently operating in the face of a heavily armed enemy, with almost no means of defending themselves against a determined attack. They roamed across the battlefield, playing a secret role they couldn't tell anyone about, employing creativity, imagination, and unorthodox thinking to save American lives. It seems right to call their efforts "laudable and glorious" and to preserve the memory of the part they played in achieving victory during World War II.

For more on continuing efforts to preserve and tell the Ghost Army story, go to www.ghostarmy.org.

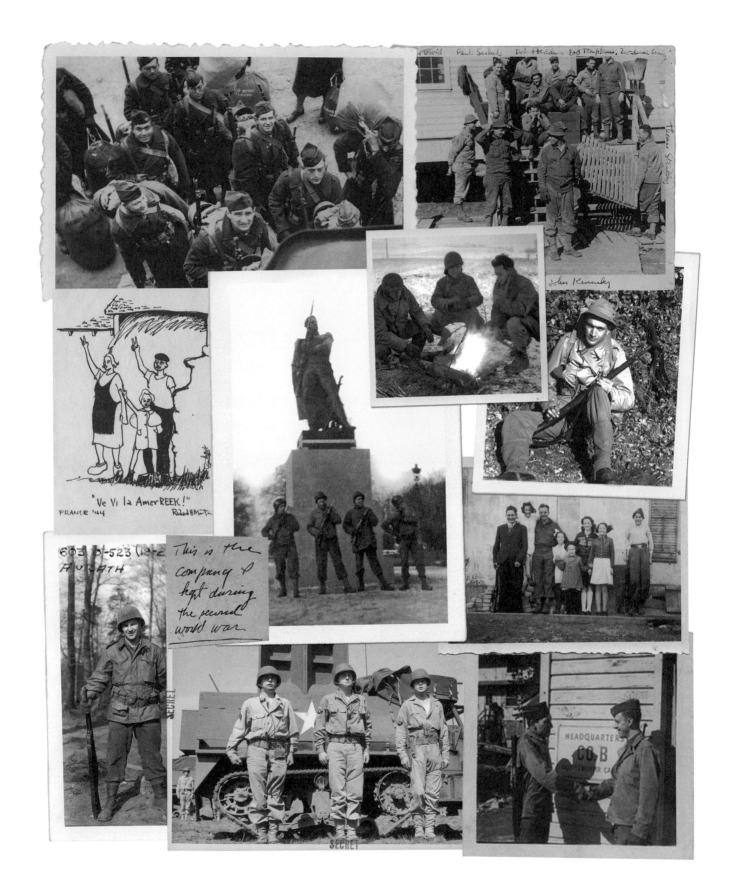

Selected Postwar Biographies

In June 1946 veterans of the 603rd attended a New York fund-raiser for Luxembourg's "Wards of the Nation" campaign. Veterans John J. Reilly (right) and Tony Cipriano (center) presented a poster they created to Andre Wolff (left), Luxembourg's Commissioner of Information. Later that year, works by Ghost Army artists went on display in Luxembourg in support of the war orphans campaign.

Al Albrecht settled in Milwaukee, Wisconsin, where he worked as a salesman for a variety of businesses, selling everything from motor homes to industrial roofing. He died in 2010 at age eighty-six.

William Anderson earned a degree as an electrical engineer and worked for a variety of companies, spending much of his time designing secret pieces of military hardware. He is retired and lives outside of Cleveland, Ohio.

Walter Arnett went to work as a staff artist for the *Louisville Courier-Journal* in 1945, and stayed there until his retirement in 1977. He died in 1998 at age eighty-six.

Spike Berry worked in radio in North Dakota, South Dakota, California, and Hawaii. He eventually started a travel business and moved to Las Vegas, Nevada. He died in 2014 at age eighty-eight.

Ed Biow had a successful career in advertising. He died in 2016, on his ninety-fifth birthday.

(left) American Pavilion guides at Expo 67 in Montreal, wearing uniforms designed by Bill Blass

(right) Bill Blass

Bill Blass became a fashion superstar. In 1970 he purchased the company where he worked as a designer and changed the name to Bill Blass Ltd., taking as a logo the mirror-image *B*s that he had once sketched on his wartime notebook. His clothes were known for their casual elegance and were worn by luminaries such as First Lady Nancy Reagan and New York socialite Brooke Astor. Blass's name became a household word, eventually appearing on everything from cars to boxes of chocolate. He was also a major fixture in New York society and known for his witty repartee and impeccable attire.

In 1945 he helped his fellow Ghost Army veteran Jack Masey get his first job. In 1967 Masey prevailed upon him to design uniforms for the United States Pavilion guides at the Expo 67 World's Fair in Montreal. Blass attended a White House dinner for Queen Elizabeth II of England in 1976, where President Gerald Ford introduced him to the queen as our "King of Fashion."

Bill Blass died in 2002 at age seventy-nine.

Edward Boccia became an expressionist painter, poet, and professor of art at Washington University in St. Louis, Missouri. He died in 2012 at age ninety-one.

Bob Boyajian worked as a staff artist for Firestone Tire and Rubber Company, then later as an ad agency creative director and photographer. He died in 2012 at age eighty-nine.

Bob Conrad practiced law for more than sixty years in New York City. He died in 2010 at age ninety.

Belisario Contreras spent twenty years working as an artist for the State Department. He received a PhD in history from American University in 1967 and wrote the book *Tradition and Innovation in New Deal Art* (1983). He died in 1990 at age seventy-three.

Harold Dahl studied sculpture under Ulric Ellerhusen. He became a fine arts appraiser and eventually owner of the Equitable Appraisal Company in New York City. He died in 1972 at age fifty-eight.

Captain Midnight, one of the comic book heroes illustrated by Victor Dowd

Victor Dowd had a wide and varied career as an artist after the war. He drew advertisements, illustrated twenty books, and spent fifteen years as a fashion illustrator. He died in 2010 at age eighty-nine.

After working for Bell Telephone Company, **Harold Flinn** took over the family farm of his wife, Ruthann, in Maquon, Illinois. Their family still owns the farm, and Harold Flinn lives not far away.

Ordained as a minister, **Fred Fox** moonlighted as a journalist, writing dozens of articles for the *New York Times*. One caught the attention of the White House, and he was brought on as an aide to President Dwight D. Eisenhower. Later Fox became the recording secretary and "Keeper of Princetonia" at his beloved alma mater, Princeton University. He died in 1981 at age sixty-three.

After the war **Barnett Greenberg** worked for the United States Postal Service, where he designed posters, signs, and stamps. He continued to paint throughout his life, donating much of his artwork to support community and religious organizations. He died in 2007 at age ninety-two.

John Hapgood's work included illustrations for the *New Yorker* and *America,* as well as ads for Bloomingdale's. He spent summers painting on Block Island, Rhode Island. He died in 1995 at age ninety.

After spending several more years on military deception, **Billy Harris** commanded the Seventh Cavalry during the Korean War and retired a major general. He died in 1986 at age seventy-five.

Ned Harris became a photographer and designer and is the author of the book *Form and Texture: A Photographic Portfolio* (1974). He was active for many years in the art community of Rockland County, New York. Ned died in 2016 at age ninety.

As an art director at a Minneapolis agency, **Cleo Hovel** dreamed up the Hamm's Beer bear, a mascot familiar to beer aficionados across the Midwest. He later worked with the legendary adman Leo Burnett. He died in 1970 at age forty-eight.

Ralph Ingersoll closed down his beloved *PM* in 1948 due to declining ad sales and political controversy. He wrote several books and became the owner of a small chain of newspapers. He died in 1985 at age eighty-four.

John Jarvie spent thirty years as an art director for Fairchild Publications, owner of *Women's Wear Daily*, supervising a staff of artists and writers. He died in 2017 at age ninety-five.

Art Kane

A visionary fashion and music photographer, **Art Kane** took the famous portrait of fifty-seven jazz musicians on a stoop in Harlem titled *Harlem 1958*. It remains a jazz icon. During the 1960s he took many arresting portraits of recording artists, including The Rolling Stones, The Doors, Bob Dylan, and Janis Joplin. His photographs of musicians, politicians, and glamorous women appeared in *Life*, *Look*, *Vogue*, *Harper's Bazaar*, and numerous other magazines. The American Society of Magazine Photographers gave Kane a lifetime achievement award in 1985. He died in 1995 at age sixty-nine.

(left) *Self Portrait, Normandy* by Ellsworth Kelly, 1944

(right) Ellsworth Kelly

Ellsworth Kelly became one of the foremost American artists of the twentieth century. In 1948 he traveled again to France, where his work evolved from figurative to abstract, inspired by shapes and pure colors. Kelly returned to New York in 1954 and soon earned an international reputation. His shaped canvases, paintings, sculptures, and prints have been exhibited in major museums around the world.

In 1973 the Museum of Modern Art in New York City mounted Kelly's first retrospective. Many more followed, including a retrospective of his sculptures at the Whitney Museum of American Art in 1982 and a 1996 career retrospective at the Solomon R. Guggenheim Museum, also in New York. His public commissions include a memorial for the United States Holocaust Memorial Museum in Washington, DC.

In 2013 President Barack Obama awarded Kelly the National Medal of Arts. "A careful observer of form, color, and the natural world," read the citation, "Mr. Kelly has shaped more than half a century of abstraction and remains a vital influence in American art."

Ellsworth Kelly lives and works in Spencertown, New York.

Harold Laynor became an art professor at Millersville University in Pennsylvania. His work has been exhibited in numerous galleries and museums. He died in 1992 at age seventy.

Joe Mack eventually started his own sales promotion business in New York City. In 1970 he retired and with his wife, Jean, founded what is now the Huntington School of Fine Arts in Greenlawn, New York. He died in 2007 at age eighty-six.

George Martin returned to his prewar employer, Schirmer Music, where he illustrated book covers, record jackets, children's books, and sheet–music covers. He died in 2007 at age ninety-one.

(left and right, top) United States Pavilion, Expo 67, Montreal

(right, bottom) The team that created the groundbreaking United States Pavilion at Expo 67. From left, Buckminster Fuller, Ghost Army veteran Jack Masey, Terry Rankine, and Peter Floyd

Jack Masey designed exhibitions around the world for the United States Information Agency. He was the director of design for the famous 1959 American National Exhibition in Moscow. The exhibit included a model American house, where Soviet Premier Nikita Khrushchev and United States Vice President Richard Nixon engaged in the so-called Kitchen Debate.

As chief of design for the American Pavilion at Expo 67 in Montreal, Masey involved many of his fellow Ghost Army artists. He enlisted Bill Blass to design the guides' uniforms, included art from Ellsworth Kelly, and commissioned a film by photographer Art Kane.

In 1979 he formed his own company, Metaform. His works include the Ellis Island Immigration Museum in New York (winner of a Presidential Design Award) and the National WWII Museum in New Orleans, among many others.

He died in 2016 at age ninety-one.

Bernie Mason spent twenty-seven years as a creative director for an ad agency and then started his own art business. He went back to school and at age seventy-five received a college degree from Villanova University. He lives outside of Philadelphia, Pennsylvania.

Irving Mayer helped design the Davy Crockett tactical nuclear weapons system. Designed for use on the battlefield, it was one of the smallest nuclear weapons systems ever built. Mayer was posthumously honored by President John F. Kennedy for his "contribution to the defense of the United States." He died in 1959 at age thirty-five.

Jack McGlynn and his wife, Helen, with Edward Kennedy, circa 1962

Jack McGlynn had a long public-service career in Massachusetts, including sixteen years as a state representative and ten years as the mayor of Medford. His son Michael followed in his footsteps as mayor. Jack McGlynn died in 2016 at age ninety-four.

Stanley Nance worked in insurance, real estate, and securities before starting his own oil-drilling company. After retiring, he led a church mission to Tahiti. Nance lives today outside Salt Lake City, Utah.

Hilton Howell Railey was awarded the Legion of Merit in 1945. He retired after the war, moving to Maine, and died in 1975 at age seventy-nine.

As a Rhodes Scholar, **George Rebh** helped establish the Oxford University Basketball Club. A career army officer, he retired a major general. He died in 2016 at age ninety-six.

Harry L Reeder was apparently removed from command of the Twenty-Third Headquarters Special Troops shortly before the end of the war. He died in 1947 at age fifty-six.

All The Creatures by William Sayles, 1955

Gil Seltzer during the war

William Sayles shared a design studio with Arthur Shilstone for several years. He illustrated many books and produced the best-selling Step-by-Step line of craft books with his wife, Shirley. Sayles died in 2018 at age ninety-eight.

With his brother Neal, **Oscar Seale** formed a manufacturers' representative firm that served the hardware industry in the Southwest for forty years. He died in 2001 at age eighty-four.

Paul Seckel was a painter and an art teacher. He married noted composer and pianist Ruth Schönthal. Their son, Al Seckel, became an internationally known authority on visual illusions. Paul Seckel died in 2013 at age ninety-five.

Gil Seltzer's career as an architect has spanned more than seventy-five years. He designed many buildings at colleges and universities, including the United States Military Academy at West Point. He is still a working architect in West Orange, New Jersey.

Alvin Shaw returned to his hometown of Annapolis, Maryland, and his prewar career as a sign painter. He died in 2005 at age ninety-six.

Arthur Shilstone's illustrations have appeared in more than thirty magazines and graced the covers of dozens of books. He was also an official NASA artist. He continues to paint in his studio in West Redding, Connecticut.

Clifford Simenson, who had hoped for an infantry command in World War II, commanded the Fourteenth Infantry Regiment in the Korean War. He later served as a military attaché in Germany. He died in 2004 at age ninety-four.

(left) Arthur Singer

(right) *Common Loons in the Mist* by Arthur Singer, 1980

Arthur Singer became one of America's best-known wildlife artists. He first made a name for himself doing illustrations for *American Home*, wildlife features for *Sports Illustrated*, and bird illustrations for *World Book Encyclopedia*. He went on to illustrate more than twenty books, including the enormously popular *Birds of the World* and *Birds of North America*. He traveled across the United States and to Africa, the Middle East, Europe, and South America to glimpse new species in their natural habits.

In 1982 he and his son Alan Singer created the "Birds and Flowers of the Fifty States" series of postage stamps. It was one of the largest-selling special issues in the history of the United States Postal Service.

Arthur Singer died in 1990 at age seventy-two.

Joe Spence had a distinguished career in arts education, finally retiring as chair of the Department of Creative Arts at the University of North Carolina. He died in 2011 at age eighty-seven.

An art professor at Tulane University's Newcomb College, **James Steg** was a noted printmaker and sculptor. His work is included in the permanent collections of more than sixty museums. He died in 2001 at age seventy-eight.

Irving Stempel worked in advertising in New York City, retired to Florida, and died in Boca Raton in 2010 at age ninety.

Dick Syracuse became a builder and a developer. The company he started with his brothers built hundreds of homes and high-rise apartments in New York and New Jersey. He died in 2013 at age ninety-one.

Bob Tompkins became an ad agency art director and design consultant. He remained lifelong friends with Bill Blass. He died in 2011 at age eighty-eight.

George Vander Sluis spent thirty-five years as an art professor at Syracuse University. In the 1960s he began painting designs on barns in upstate New York to encourage preservation efforts. He died in 1984 at age sixty-nine.

John Walker spent thirty years in the United States Army. A highly decorated officer, he saw action in Korea and Vietnam before retiring as full colonel. He died in 2010 at age ninety.

Keith Williams's promising career as an artist was cut short when he died in 1951 at age forty-six. His etchings and paintings are represented in the collections of the Library of Congress and the New-York Historical Society among others.

Stanley M. Wright had, in his own words, "a wonderful adventure" as northern Vermont's foremost impressionist painter and founder of the Wright School of Art in Stowe. He died in 1996 at age eighty-four.

Tony Young worked at Peoples Gas in Chicago, retiring as advertising manager after forty-four years. He continued to study art on his own, working in a variety of media. He died in 2009 at age eighty-seven.

A number of other Ghost Army artists who do not appear in this book also had notable careers. **George Dietsel** and **Otis Riggs** designed sets for Broadway and Hollywood. **Eddie Haas** was the cocreator of the 1960s TV show *The Munsters*. **George Nardiello** was a fashion designer who created dresses for Marilyn Monroe. **Bud Bier** designed packaging for Dentyne and Chiclets chewing gum. Architect **James Jackson** was part of the team that worked on the Space Needle, in Seattle. And there were many more.

Three Ghost Army soldiers never came home. Captain **Thomas Wells**, Sergeant **George Peddle**, and Corporal **Chester Pelliccioni** all made the ultimate sacrifice to help win the war.

Five Ghost Army veterans. From left, Jack Masey, Ned Harris, Tom Roche, William Sayles, and John Jarvie

Sources and Notes

Ghost Army Veteran Interviews

By far the most important source for both *The Ghost Army* documentary and this book were the men of Twenty-Third Headquarters Special Troops. Between 2005 and 2012, Rick Beyer conducted interviews with twenty-two of them: Al Albrecht, Spike Berry, Ed Biow, Bob Conrad, Victor Dowd, Harold Flinn, Ned Harris, John Jarvie, Jack Masey, Bernie Mason, Jack McGlynn, Stanley Nance, George Rebh, William Sayles, Gil Seltzer, Arthur Shilstone, Adolphus "Ace" Simpson, Joe Spence, Irving Stempel, Dick Syracuse, Bob Tompkins, and John Walker.

Additional Author Interviews

Ray Bacon, codirector, Museum of Work and Culture, Woonsocket, RI; Dr. Leo Beranek, former director, Electro-Acoustic Lab at Harvard University (one of many credits in a distinguished scientific career); General Wesley Clark, former commander of NATO; Roy Eichhorn, director of research at the United States Army Combined Arms Center; Jonathan Gawne, author, *Ghosts of the ETO* (2002); and Theresa Ricard, former employee, U.S. Rubber. Additional Ricard interview material was graciously provided by documentary filmmaker Tim Grey.

Unpublished Letters and Manuscripts

The most important document for anyone chronicling the Ghost Army is "The Official History of the 23rd Headquarters Special Troops," by Frederic Fox, which can be found at the National Archives in College Park, Maryland. It was classified for nearly forty years after the war. It may be the most entertaining official unit history ever written by an officer of the United States Army.

Another important source is "The History of Company A, 293rd Engineer Battalion, 406th Engineer Combat Company Special," written by Corporal Rolff Campbell, with the help of other soldiers in the unit. The manuscript of this very unofficial unit history was made available by General George Rebh, commander of the 406th Combat Engineers.

The handwritten diary of Bob Tompkins, typed up by Bill Blass's mother, is unique among Ghost Army primary source materials in that it offers an unofficial, uncensored glimpse of what soldiers were thinking and feeling while they were conducting operations. Tompkins generously made the diary available.

Ralph Ingersoll wrote extensively about his involvement with the Ghost Army in "Time Out for War," an unpublished manuscript that is now part of the Ralph Ingersoll Collection at the Howard Gotlieb Archival Research Center at Boston University. Most of his quotes come from this document.

Three prolific Ghost Army letter writers were Harold Dahl, Fred Fox, and Harold Laynor. Dahl's letters to his mother and sister were painstakingly transcribed by his daughter, Janet Carolyn Freeman, and run to nearly five hundred pages. Fox compiled his letters, with some interstitial comment, into a manuscript titled "Instant Army"; his son, Reverend Donald Fox, generously shared it with the authors. Laynor's letters were made available by his wife, Gloria Laynor.

Additional Letters and Manuscripts

Anderson, William. "Code Name: Blarney, The Story About the 23d Hdqtrs. Spl. Troops." Unpublished manuscript courtesy of its author.

Dondelinger, Anny. Letter to Stanley Wright's father. May 20, 1945. Courtesy of James Saslow.

Eldredge, H. Wentworth. Partial autobiography. Milne Special Collections and Archives, University of New Hampshire Library, Durham, NH.

Geisel, Theodore. Wartime diary. November–December 1945. The Dr. Seuss Collection, Mandeville Special Collections, Geisel Library, University of California, San Diego.

Harris, Colonel William, Major Ralph Ingersoll, and Captain Wentworth Eldredge. "Informal Report by Special Plans Branch to Joint Security Control, 25 May, 1945." College Park, MD: National Archives.

The Laynor Foundation Museum. *An Artist Goes to War.* Documentary film about Harold Laynor. Gigantic Productions: 1992. Courtesy of Gloria Laynor.

Patten, Robert. "Fred Patten, His Family Biography and Life Story." Unpublished manuscript courtesy of its author.

Simenson, Colonel Clifford. "World War II: My Story after Fifty Years." 1995. Washington, DC: U.S. Army Center of Military History.

Wright, Stanley. Letter to his mother. May 8, 1945. Courtesy of James Saslow.

Plus articles from *US* (U.S. Rubber's in-house magazine), courtesy of Bob Tompkins and of the Museum of Work and Culture, Woonsocket, RI; various United States Army memos and reports from the National Archives, College Park, MD; and various United States Army memos and reports collected by and courtesy of Roy Eichhorn.

Additional documents are gathered in the Ghost Army Digital Archive.

Articles

Arnett, John W. "The Ghost Army Days of Walter Arnett." Website of the Crescent Hill Baptist Church, Louisville, KY. Accessed January 16, 2013. http://www.chbc-lky.org/arnettforest/wendell-ghostarmydays.htm.

Boyanowski, Henry. "Ghost Army Fools Foe in Neatest Trick of War." *Worcester Daily Telegram*. August 29, 1945.

Dudley, Fred W. "Lowell Factory Made One of War's Most Fantastic Weapons." *Lowell Sun*. February 13, 1946.

Gyongy, Adrienne. "Faking Out the Enemy." *Prattfolio* (Fall 2008): 12–17.

Kronman, Mark. "The Deceptive Practices of the 23rd Special Headquarters, Special Troop during World War II." Aberdeen, MD: Aberdeen Proving Ground Tactical Operations Office (January 1978). Accessed through the U.S. Army Center of Military History.

New York Times. "Army Reveals use of 'Ghost Army' in War; Pneumatic Decoys Misled Foe, Won Battles." December 5, 1945.

Park, Edwards. "A Phantom Division Played a Role in Germany's Defeat." *Smithsonian* 16, no. 1 (April 1985): 138–47.

Books

Blass, Bill, and Cathy Horyn. *Bare Blass*. New York: HarperCollins, 2003.

Blumenson, Martin. *The Patton Papers, 1940–1945*. Boston: Houghton Mifflin, 1974.

Delmer, Sefton. *The Counterfeit Spy*. New York: Harper & Row, 1971.

Deutsch, Harold C., and John Mendelsohn. *Basic Deception and the Normandy Invasion*. New York: Garland Publishing, 1989.

Eisenhower, John. *The Bitter Woods: The Battle of the Bulge*. New York: G. P. Putnam's Sons, 1969.

Foote, Shelby. *The Civil War: A Narrative, Volume 1*. New York: Random House, 1958.

Ford, Mark Morgan. *America in Still Life: Barnett Greenberg*. New York: Cap & Bells Press, 2012.

Gawne, Jonathan. *Ghosts of the ETO: American Tactical Deception Units in the European Theater, 1944–1945*. Havertown, PA: Casemate Publishers, 2002.

Gerard, Philip. *Secret Soldiers: The Story of World War II's Heroic Army of Deception*. New York: Dutton, 2002.

Gilmore, Donald L., ed. *U.S. Army Atlas of the European Theater in World War II*. New York: Barnes & Noble Publishing, 2004.

Goossen, E. C. *Ellsworth Kelly*. New York: Museum of Modern Art, 1973.

Holt, Thaddeus. *The Deceivers: Allied Military Deception in the Second World War*. New York: Scribner, 2004.

Hoopes, Roy. *Ralph Ingersoll: A Biography*. New York: Atheneum, 1985.

McCullough, David. *1776*. Dumfries, NC: Holt, McDougal, 2006.

Praun, Albert. *German Radio Intelligence and the Soldatensender*. Washington, DC: Department of the Army, Office of the Chief of Military History, 1950.

Note on Rank

Military rank can change both up and down and is bewildering in its arcane detail. We have tried to keep things simple for the telling of the story. In most cases, we have used the highest rank that the person attained during the war, as best as we can determine. In the case of soldiers who served as technicians (ranks T/3 through T/5), we have used the more common appellation of Sergeant or Corporal. We did not distinguish among different levels of Sergeant (such as Staff Sergeant, First Sergeant, and so on). Two of the men central to this tale, Ralph Ingersoll and Fred Fox, were promoted during their time in Europe, and the story reflects that.

Acknowledgments

We owe a deep debt of gratitude to all the veterans of the Ghost Army who have generously shared their stories and their art, which made possible the telling of the tale:

Al Albrecht, Bill Anderson, Walter Arnett, A. G. "Spike" Berry, Bud Bier, Ed Biow, Bill Blass, Edward Boccia, John Borders, Bob Boyajian, Bob Conrad, Belisario Contreras, Mordecai Reese Craig, Harold Dahl, Victor Dowd, Harold Flinn, Fred Fox, Barnett Greenberg, John Hapgood, Ned Harris, Cleo Hovel, John Jarvie, Art Kane, Ellsworth Kelly, John Kennedy, Harold Laynor, Nick Leo, Joseph Mack, George Martin, Jack Masey, Bernie Mason, Irving Mayer, Jack McGlynn, Richard Morton, Stanley Nance, Gazo Nemeth, Seymour Nussbaum, Marion Pastorcich, George Rebh, Tom Roche, William Sayles, Paul Seckel, Gil Seltzer, Alvin Shaw, Arthur Shilstone, Adolphus "Ace" Simpson, Leonard Simms, Arthur Singer, Joe Spence, James Steg, Irving Stempel, Dick Syracuse, Bob Tompkins, George Vander Sluis, John Walker, Keith Shaw Williams, Stanley Wright, Tony Young, and Bruce Zillmer.

We would like to thank the families of the veterans who searched through their attics and archives to retrieve, scan, and deliver unto us the artwork, photos, and writings of their loved ones:

Holly Anderson, John Arnett, Beth Barham, Jocelyn Craig Benzaia, Rosa Bland, Alice Boccia, Bob Borders, Gail Boyajian, Kat Butler, Marta Contreras, Dylan Craig, Nate Dahl, Gregory Dowd, Peter Dowd, Roy Eichhorn, Claudia Fenderson, Rev. Donald Fox, Janet Carolyn Freeman, Clifford Harris, Richard Hovel, Jonathan Kane, Lynn Kennedy, Gloria Laynor, Stephen Mack, Rob Mayer, Pamela Pastoric, Linda Phillips, James Saslow, Michael Sayles, Jan Seale, Kim Seale, Al Seckel, Bart Shaw, Alan Singer, Paul Singer, Carol Spence, Mary Spence, Frances Swigart-Steg, Rina Syracuse, Andrea Syracuse-Silverstein, Jeff Vander Sluis, and Erika Vrabel.

Thanks also to Irene Blais, Peter Harrington, Karl F. Jackson, David Howe, Kevin Koloff, Jessica Kurrle, Jim Levine, Bob Patten, Scott Patti, Eva Walters, and Paul Webber. Special thanks to Roy Eichhorn, former director of research and development at the United States Army Combined Arms Center, for reviewing the manuscript. Any errors that remain are ours, not his.

We are grateful to Princeton Architectural Press, especially acquisitions editor Sara Bader for championing the book, project editor Sara Stemen for her thorough and judicious use of the comments tool in Word, copy editor Tanya Heinrich for her exacting attention to detail, and designer Benjamin English for making art out of all the raw material. Together they made the book practically perfect.

This book grew out of the documentary film *The Ghost Army*, written and directed by Rick Beyer, which premiered on PBS in 2013. We would like to thank everyone involved in the making of that film, especially Martha Gavin, Mark Tomizawa, and Jacqueline Sheridan. From PBS, thanks to Beth Hoppe, Cara Liebenson, Amy Letourneau, Charles Schuerhoff, and Jalyn Henton. And our grateful appreciation goes to the generous donors who supported production of the film and continue to support the creation of a Ghost Army Digital Archive.

Many original art pieces that appear in this book were collected for several exhibitions of the art of the Ghost Army. We would like to thank Clare Sheridan, Joanne Potanovic, and the Board of the Historical Society of Rockland County, as well as Carole Perry and the Board of the Edward Hopper House Art Center in Nyack, New York.

Finally we would like to acknowledge our spouses, Marilyn Rea Beyer and Matt Dow, and thank them for their patience, support, enthusiasm, and love.

— *Rick Beyer & Elizabeth Sayles*

Credits

Grateful acknowledgment is made to the following for permission to extensively quote from unpublished material:

The family of Harold Dahl for his letters.

Gloria Laynor for Harold Laynor's letters.

The Ingersoll Collection, Howard Gotleib Archival Research Center at Boston University, for Ralph Ingersoll's unpublished manuscript *Time Out for War.*

Mark Tompkins for Bob Tompkins's diaries.

James Saslow for Stanley Wright's letter.

Image credits:

Al Seckel: 164 right.

Alan & Paul Singer: Cover top; 29 bottom; 56 bottom; 77; 78; 111; 125 top right; 159 bottom; 175 bottom; 185; 203; 238.

Alice Boccia: 84 bottom; 212 left.

Arthur Shilstone: 57; 66 top; 67; 69 top; 85 bottom; 96; 97; 117 bottom; 121 left.

Anne S. K. Brown Military Collection / Brown University Library: 26; 55 top; 79 right; 92; 107 right; 118 left; 130; 131; 133 left; 164 left; 174 top; 175 top; 183; 204 bottom; 229 second row left.

Bart Shaw & Elizabeth S. Barham: 115; 202.

Bernie Mason: 30 top; 38; 62; 136; 165 left; 207 right.

Bill Blass Group: 30 bottom; 176 bottom; 231 right.

Bob Boyajian: 12 second row left; 28; 39 right; 149; 172;

229 second row lower right.

Bob Tompkins 14; 36; 38; 84 top; 93 top; 106 top left; 121 right; 125 bottom; 127 right; 176 top; 194 bottom.

Carol Spence: 187 right.

Chermayeff & Geismar: 235 left & top right.

Comicbook Plus / Fawcett: 232.

David Howe: 173 top.

Dick Syracuse: 12 second row right; 117 top.

Dr. Paul Webber: 200.

Ed Biow: 102; 155 bottom.

Ellsworth Kelly: 31 top; 39 left; 55 bottom left; 98; 179; 184; 210; 234.

Erika Vrabel: 32 top left; 163 left; 193 bottom.

The family of Harold Dahl: 12 top left, third row middle, bottom left & right; 51; 129; 132 right; 150; 154; 220; 229 top left & third row right; 230.

Frances Steg: 118 right; 174 middle; 212 right.

George Rebh: 45.

Gilbert Seltzer: 237 bottom.

Gloria Laynor: 180.

The Ingersoll Collection, Howard Gotlieb Archival Research Center at Boston University: 16.

Irene Blais: 41 bottom.

Jack Masey: 35; 231 left; 235 bottom right.

Jack McGlynn: 12 third row left & right; 47; 236.

James Saslow: 166–169.

Jeff Vander Sluis: 40; 120 top; 137; 177 left; 239 top.

John Arnett: 133 top & bottom right; 134.

John Jarvie: 32 top right; 43 bottom; 54; 76 right & left; 79 left; 122; 157; 174 bottom; 177 right; 207 left.

Jonathan Kane & Holly Anderson: 233.

Leo Beranek: 49.

Leonard Simms: 136 top; 170; 206.

Library of Congress: 24.

Linda Philips: 104; 107 left; 156 top right; 161.

Marta Contreras: 75 bottom;

130; 175 top; 204 bottom.

Museum of Work and Culture: 42.

Michael Sayles: 83 top.

National Archives: Cover bottom; 2–3; 11; 18; 19; 41 top; 46; 48; 58; 63; 64 bottom; 71; 75 top; 80; 86; 87; 88; 93 bottom; 94; 95; 105 top; 112; 116; 119; 151; 153; 191; 192; 194 top left & right; 195; 196; 199; 214; 221; 229 bottom left & middle.

The National World War II Museum: 228.

Ned Harris: 65; 66 bottom; 120 bottom; 127 left; 159 top; 178 left; 204 top; 213.

P. C. Hamerlinck: 27.

Pamela Pastoric: 219.

Peter Dowd: 29 top right & left; 52; 55 bottom right; 56 top; 64 top; 90; 106 top right & bottom left; 109; 125 top left; 132 left; 156 bottom left & right; 163 right; 205 left; 209; 211; 217 bottom.

Rev. Donald Fox: 21; 83 bottom.

Richard Hovel: 100.

Rick Beyer: 6; 7; 13; 31 bottom; 43 top; 85 top; 239 bottom; 254.

Rob Mayer: 70; 155 top; 156 top left; 173 bottom; 181; 188; 190; 198; 229 second row third from left.

Roy Eichhorn: 22–23; 32 bottom; 105 bottom; 126; 186; 216; 226; 227.

Spike Berry: 135.

Stanley Nance: 44; 124; 193 top.

Steve Mack 13; 33; 50; 72; 146; 162; 165 bottom right.

William Anderson: 108.

William Sayles: 12 top right; 59; 60; 69 bottom; 101; 106 bottom right; 110; 128; 139–145; 165 top right; 205 right; 217 top; 218; 229 top right, center & bottom right; 237 top.

Worcester Telegram & Gazette: 225.

Index

About the Authors

Rick Beyer is a best-selling author, an award-winning documentary filmmaker, and a longtime history enthusiast.

Beyer first heard about the Ghost Army in 2005 and began work on an independent documentary film about the unit, *The Ghost Army*, which premiered on PBS in 2013. He has also made documentary films for History, National Geographic Channel, A&E, the Smithsonian Institution, and many others.

He is the author of the popular The Greatest Stories Never Told series of history books, described by the *Chicago Tribune* as "an old-fashioned sweetshop full of tasty morsels."

Beyer and his wife, Marilyn Rea Beyer, live in Lexington, Massachusetts.

Ghost Army veterans John Jarvie, Ned Harris, and William Sayles (left to right) pose near a fake tank prop with the authors, Elizabeth Sayles and Rick Beyer, at the opening of the *Art of the Ghost Army* exhibition at the Historical Society of Rockland County, in New City, New York, in 2011.

Elizabeth Sayles is an award-winning illustrator of children's books. She has illustrated more than twenty-nine books, including *I Already Know I Love You* by Billy Crystal, a *New York Times* bestseller, as well as *The Goldfish Yawned*, which she also wrote.

Sayles grew up on stories of the Ghost Army told by her father, William Sayles. She worked with Rick Beyer to curate an exhibition of Ghost Army art at the Edward Hopper House Art Center in Nyack, New York, one of many art shows she has cocurated.

Sayles is an adjunct professor of illustration at the School of Visual Arts in New York City and at the City University of New York, Queens.

She lives in the lovely Hudson Valley, New York, with her husband, Matt Dow, and their daughter, Jessica.

Published by
Princeton Architectural Press
202 Warren Street, Hudson, New York 12534
www.papress.com

Editor: Sara E. Stemen
Designer: Benjamin English

Special thanks to:
Meredith Baber, Sara Bader, Nicola Bednarek Brower,
Janet Behning, Erin Cain, Megan Carey, Carina Cha,
Andrea Chlad, Tom Cho, Barbara Darko, Russell Fernandez,
Jan Cigliano Hartman, Jan Haux, Mia Johnson, Diane Levinson,
Jennifer Lippert, Katharine Myers, Jaime Nelson, Rob Shaeffer,
Marielle Suba, Kaymar Thomas, Paul Wagner, Joseph Weston,
and Janet Wong of Princeton Architectural Press
—Kevin C. Lippert, publisher

Library of Congress Cataloging-in-Publication Data:
Beyer, Rick, 1956–
The Ghost Army of World War II : how one top-secret unit
deceived the enemy with inflatable tanks, sound effects, and
other audacious fakery / Rick Beyer and Elizabeth Sayles.
253 pages : illustrations, maps; 26 cm.
Includes index.
ISBN 978-1-61689-318-7 (alk. paper)
1. United States. Army. Headquarters Special Troops, 23rd.
2. World War, 1939–1945—Campaigns—Western Front.
3. World War, 1939–1945—Deception—United States.
4. Disinformation—United States—History. 5. World War,
1939–1945—Regimental histories—United States.
I. Sayles, Elizabeth. II. Title.
D769.25.B49 2014
940.54'8673—dc23   2014027598

This image is taken from
the hand-painted cover of
the *Official History of the
23rd Headquarters Special
Troops*, written by Captain
Fred Fox in 1945 and now
at the National Archives. The
Twenty-Third had no official
insignia since they were a
secret deception unit.

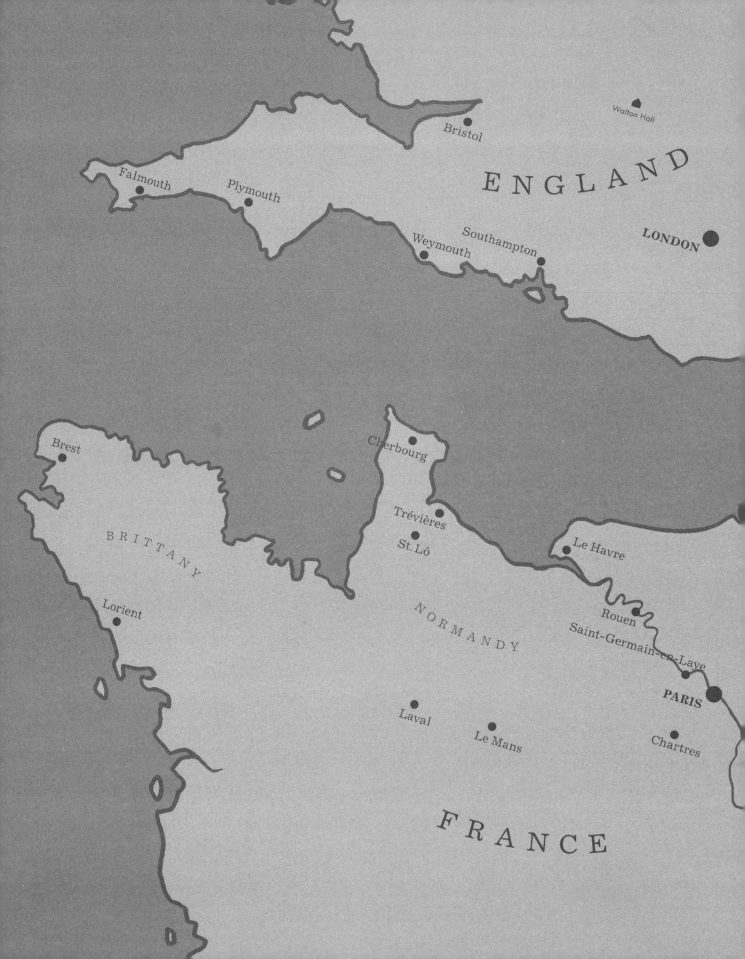